THE ART OF FILO COOKBOOK

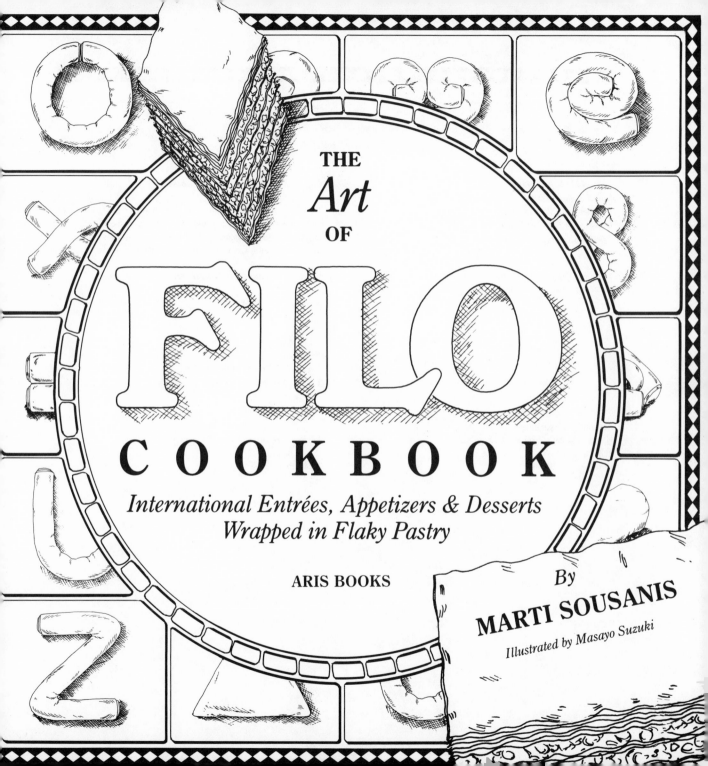

THE *Art* OF
FILO
COOKBOOK

International Entrées, Appetizers & Desserts
Wrapped in Flaky Pastry

ARIS BOOKS

By
MARTI SOUSANIS

Illustrated by Masayo Suzuki

Produced by L. John Harris
Edited by Sherry Virbila
Contributing editor: Charles Perry
Cover design by Jeanne Jambu
Typesetting by Accent & Alphabet

The binding of this book has been Smyth sewn
for strength and easy opening.

Aris Books are published by
Harris Publishing Company, Inc.
1635 Channing Way
Berkeley, CA 94703

Library of Congress Cataloging in Publication Data

Sousanis, Marti, 1943–
    The art of filo.

    Includes indexes.
        1. Cookery (Filo dough) 2. Cookery, Greek.
    3. Cookery, Near Eastern.   I. Title.
    TX770.S68 1982   641.8   83-3917

    ISBN 0-943186-05-6 (pbk.)

Manufactured in the United States of America
2   4   6   8   9   7   5   3
First printing June 1983

Στόν πατέρα μου μέ τήν ἀγάπη μου

TABLE OF CONTENTS

PART III — RECIPES 57

ACKNOWLEDGMENTS

This is it — the time to acknowledge all of you filophiles who have contributed to the book in one way or another and encouraged me to "fool around with filo."

For their support, encouragement, enthusiasm and tastings, I must thank my dear family — Dean and Anne Sousanis, their children John, Dan and Nick (who were always eager to assist in the kitchen, provided they could stick their fingers into the experiment at hand); Rosalie Sempliner for always sharing her recipes, ideas and love; Saichi Kawahara for his critical editorial advice and his relentless efforts at trying to teach a Greek egomaniac to be "a little more humble."

The artist, Masayo Suzuki, cannot be overlooked in this list. Without her fine illustrations, this book would not have been complete. She is to be commended for her admirable flexibility in dropping everything (upon one long-distance phone call) to respond to a mad Greek's insistence that, "This book must be done, and it must be done immediately." After agreeing to this job (with no money and no publisher in sight), Masayo graciously invited me to come to Hawaii to begin the book and then had the fortitude to put up with me for an entire month in her home (an impossible feat for most).

Special thanks go to Hal Lum for his encouragement of Masayo and me; Mitchell Waite for his generous and sound business advice; Henry Dakin for his warm generosity; Diane Dexter, who makes the art of home filo-making look easy; George Stoyanof of Stoyanof's Cafe and Restaurant, Migirdich Sagatelyan and his brother, Mihran, of Sheherazade Bakery, who generously shared their knowledge and expertise in the art of commercial filo-making; Mimi Luebbermann for her cheerful and uncomplaining assistance, which was a tremendous help to me in the Aris Kitchen; D. Novella Bruner for all of her help and patience; Tim Ware for his helpful copyediting; Ed Chu for demonstrating Hawaiian hospitality by loaning a total stranger his expensive electric typewriter; Lambis Apostolopoulos, of Greek-American Food Imports, for answering all my questions;

Moncef Jaziri and countless others who have shared their recipes with me over the years.

My enthusiastic (and not so enthusiastic) tasters should be recognized. For the most zealous of my devotees, the award goes to Liz Walker and Jon Katz (who, when asked for suggestions and critiques, responded only with moans and groans of delight; while not very helpful, they were inspirational). This list also includes: Jo Kawahara Olson and Al Olson, Cara and Sean Dana, Faith and Fred Seal, Sheila and Gardner Bride, and Dmitri Katz — all of whom were fervent supporters of this filomania; Roberta Moore and Joe Mays (who even liked my flops); Kathy Kelly (who didn't like my flops); and JoEllyn Taylor, who flew to Hawaii specifically to drive me crazy with her prolific, madcap suggestions for titles of this book, among which were "Touchy Filo" and "Filosophy."

I was very fortunate to have Sherry Virbila as my editor. Her contributions were invaluable and I appreciated her patience, good humor and suggestions.

Finally, I'd like to say a word about my publisher, John Harris (who happens to love garlic as much as I do). How many authors are lucky enough to have a "hell of a decent guy" for a publisher (not to mention funny, warm, down-to-earth and quite open to ideas and suggestions from his authors)? Well, New York, I'm not sure I could have had all that with you! There's something nice about breaking bread (or should I say "breaking filo") with your publisher every week, while testing recipes in his kitchen, that creates an open, trusting and symbiotic relationship.

Thank you all.

INTRODUCTION

Filo, Phyllo, Fillo — any way it's spelled, it is all the same: a delicate, light and flaky pastry. Filo means "leaf" in Greek and that describes the paper-thin quality of the pastry. It can be used for appetizers, lunch or dinner dishes, as well as fabulous desserts. Traditionally, filo has been used throughout the Middle East, and you can always find filo dough in Greek, Armenian and Middle Eastern delicatessens and markets.   More and more grocery stores, markets and specialty shops carry filo. Using ready-made filo requires less preparation time for each recipe than if you make the wrappings from scratch. Yet there is a delight in making one's own filo, and the recipe on page 26 will explain to you the art of making filo dough.

The purpose of this book is to introduce you to the infinite variety of international dishes and creative shapes possible with filo. You will discover how enjoyable and easy it is to work with. When you begin to explore the possibilities, you'll find yourself creating new recipes and artistic forms of your own. You can substitute filo for the outer wrapping of any stuffed dish from around the world — Chinese *wonton* skins and eggrolls, Mexican *tortillas,* Indonesian and Philippine *lumpia,* Russian *piroshki,* Argentinian *empanadas,* French *crepes,* Japanese *gyoza* — the list is endless. As a result of the variety of shapes and fillings that can be made, you will be delighted with the elegant and delicious creations you produce.

Having grown up in a Greek home, I was familiar with filo only in such dishes as *baklava* (pages 117–118) and *spanakopita* (pages 67–68). I was somewhat intimidated by filo until my Polish friend, Zinki, showed me how easy it is to work with. Over the years, as I taught Greek and Middle Eastern cooking classes, I began to experiment with filo in unorthodox ways. First, I would demonstrate the traditional dishes and shapes. Then, I'd encourage my students to try new shapes, suggesting even simple *origami* shapes taken from the Japanese art of paper-folding. What began as straightforward cooking classes evolved into creative food workshops as my enthusiastic students became appropriately irreverent with filo and began to explore new possibilities.

I do hope my book will dispel some of the mystique of filo and encourage you to create with it. You will be pleased with the elegant results. Any suggestions you may have for new recipes and shapes, or for improving this book, I welcome. Please submit them through my publisher.

Marti Sousanis
San Francisco, California

HISTORICAL INTRODUCTION

Filo, as we know it, was invented about five hundred years ago, but its roots go back at least another five hundred years. This thousand-year history is as convoluted and multilayered as the original and most popular expression of filo, *baklava*. We all know *baklava* as that delicious pastry available at Greek restaurants and delis, but its ultimate origins go far beyond Greece into Central Asia, for filo was invented by the Turks.

When the Turks first appeared in history (around the seventh century) they were wandering nomads, but surprisingly they did know of agriculture and grain played a large part in their diet. One of the two dozen or so flour-based foods they ate was a thin unleavened bread, similar to a Mexican tortilla, that was fried on a simple iron sheet the Turks used for all their baking. This bread was called *yufka,* the same word the Turks use today for a single sheet of filo. Often the Turks served *yufkas* folded or piled up in stacks with butter or other fillings between the layers. "Folded bread" is one of the definitions given for the word in an eleventh century dictionary.

But these stacked *yufkas* did not evolve into filo until after the Turks entered the Near East in the tenth century and came into contact with the refined cookery of the Moslem courts. Here an early form of puff paste was in use, made much as we make puff paste today: a slab of dough is covered with butter, folded over several times and rolled thin. The layers within this folded dough, separated by films of butter, are far thinner than one could make by rolling alone.

At first this type of pastry was not at all to the Turks' liking. After his Persian courtiers presented him with almond-stuffed pastry made with puff paste, an early sultan commented, "These are good noodles, but they need garlic." (The world is always shocked, as these Persians were, by the idea of a sweet dish with garlic. The Persian expression for a "fly in the ointment" is "garlic in the *baklava.*")

A few centuries later, when the Turks had become more cosmopolitan, Sultan Mehmet III conquered Constantinople, renamed it Istanbul and inaugurated a great age of official patronage of the arts —

including cookery. Filo is not something that is made by accident; it had to be invented by a specialist. Almost certainly it was in the vast kitchens of the Topkapi Palace in Istanbul, with its armies of cooks and pastrymakers, that someone stretched the traditional *yufka* until it was as thin as a layer in puff paste.

This first filo dish appears to have been *baklava,* which became a symbol of the good life to the Turks. In the middle 1500s Sultan Suleyman the Magnificent instituted a ceremony called the Baklava Procession to reward his palace guard, the Janissaries. On one particular day of the year huge trays of *baklava* were presented to the Janissaries, who carried them back from Topkapi to their barracks in a grand procession. In the eighteenth and nineteenth centuries filo was such a passion with the Turks that the great houses of Istanbul always employed two filo makers: one to make *yufka* for *baklava* and another to make a slightly different (probably sturdier) kind for pastries called *börek* (see page 105).

Soon after Suleyman the Magnificent invaded Hungary, people there started writing about a pastry called *rétes,* the first recorded name for strudel, and *yufka* had begun its European career. The Asian and African colonies of the Ottoman Empire also developed filo pastries of their own, and the world has continued to experiment with this fascinating pastry dough. It is the most versatile way of making a pastry that is rich and at the same time light and delicate. This is quite a tribute to a descendant of a bread nomads cooked over grass fires in Central Asia a thousand years ago.

Historical background provided by Charles Perry from his paper "Grain Foods of the Ancient Turks," delivered at the Oxford Symposium, St. Antony's College, June 24–26, 1983.

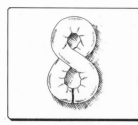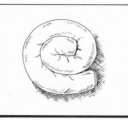

PART ONE

PRELIMINARIES

A GUIDE TO USING THIS BOOK

1. It is important that you read all the material in this section before trying to work with filo.

2. Read through the entire recipe and instructions for the shape *before* you begin preparation.

3. The only tools you will need are a good pastry brush, a pair of scissors and a very sharp knife.

4. The shapes indicated for each recipe are only suggestions. You may use *any* shape you desire for *any* recipe — they're all interchangeable. However, the shape that you decide to use for any given filling will determine whether the dish can be used as an appetizer, side dish or main entrée. For example, the smaller shapes, such as triangles or short rolls, are ideal for appetizers and the larger shapes are suitable for main courses.

5. You may use any filling from other sources that you wish, but when creating your own fillings be sure you precook any pork, sausage, chicken or other meats you use.

6. Once you have mastered the "art of filo," create your own shapes and fillings.

7. Remember, almost any stuffed dish from around the world can be adapted for filo, especially if it calls for a pastry wrapping, such as puff paste or parchment paper. Filo is neutral in taste, so it can usually go with almost anything.

Important Note: Remember, each recipe in the book is made up of two parts: a filling recipe and a shape instruction. After completing the filling recipe, turn to the shape section to wrap or layer your filling with filo.

IMPORTANT TIPS ON WORKING WITH FILO

1. It's always best to work with fresh filo, if it is available. However, if you're using frozen filo, read the section on "Storing and Freezing Filo" (page 21).

2. Have 1 package (1 pound) of commercial filo on hand for all the recipes, even though most recipes do not require a full pound. There are approximately 18 to 20 sheets of filo in a 1-pound package, each sheet measuring about 12 inches by 20 inches. The number of filo sheets needed for any recipe varies somewhat because each filo maker uses more or less filling per pastry than the amount specified in the recipe. A pound of filo will ensure that you have enough and the extra sheets can be frozen and used later (see page 21).

3. Never work in direct sunlight or heat; filo tends to dry out quickly.

4. Your work surface should be dry or the filo will stick to it.

5. Try to work as quickly as possible. Otherwise, cover the filo with a slightly damp towel or plastic wrap, or put the filo that you aren't immediately using in the refrigerator.

6. Use scissors or a very sharp knife to cut the filo.

7. Shake off any excess cornstarch.

8. If the filo is too dry and starts to crack while you're working with it, try misting it very lightly with water.

9. If the filo sheets stick together slightly, gently shake them and slowly peel them apart along the edges. If, however, you cannot separate the sheets, leave them together and brush a little more generously with butter or oil.

10. Hopefully this won't be the case, but if the filo you are using is not in good condition, return it immediately to the store where you purchased it and ask that your money be returned. However, if you cannot do this and must work with what you have, you can attempt a "patchwork quilt" technique. Simply take the torn or stuck-together bits and pieces of filo and patch them together by overlapping them until you have a complete layer. Be sure to grease the sheets generously so they will blend together smoothly. This will take time and patience, but the end result will be acceptable.

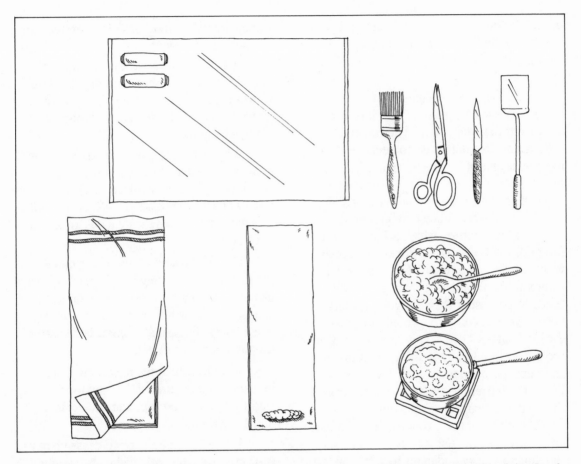

Equipment needed for making filo: baking sheet, brush, scissors, knife, spatula, towel, mixing bowls.

11. Always use a good, natural bristle pastry brush or paint brush (at least 1½- to 2-inches wide) for brushing filo.

12. Brush filo with only a very small amount of butter or oil. Cover the entire surface and remember not to neglect the edges. If you use an excessive amount, your pastry will be too greasy; if you don't use enough, it will be too dry. Moderation is the key here.

13. When the recipe calls for unsalted butter instead of regular butter, it is very important that you use it. The recipes that call for unsalted butter do so because numerous layers of filo are being used, as in *baklava*. If you use regular, salted butter, the salt content increases noticeably and causes the delicate pastry to be ruined.

Clarified butter, which is butter with the milk solids removed, works extremely well with filo. As a result of the milk solids' removal, the filo never gets soggy and it tends to be crisper than if regular unclarified butter were used. If you would rather use clarified butter, here is how to make it. Cut the butter into small pieces (to melt faster) and heat it in a saucepan over low heat. When the butter has melted, remove from the heat and skim the foam from the top. Then, put the butter through a fine strainer into a bowl. Let it rest for a few minutes, allowing the milky sediment to settle on the bottom. The clear yellow liquid sitting on the top is the butter fat. Carefully transfer just the butter fat to another container, leaving the sediment behind.

14. Oven temperatures frequently vary. A good oven thermometer is useful; however, the best way of judging when your pastry is done is by the color. It should always be golden brown.

15. After the pastry is baked or fried, allow it to cool a bit before cutting (most recipes indicate the cooling time). Then, use a very sharp, thin-bladed knife to cut with, as the pastry is so delicate a dull knife will shred it to pieces.

16. The easiest (and, in my opinion, the best) way of eating any filo pastry is to pick it up with your hands and eat it like a sandwich. Using a fork mutilates such delicate pastry. Place a few finger bowls around the table for your guests.

17. To reheat filo pastry, wrap it loosely in aluminum foil, leaving the foil slightly open at the top, and place it in a 350°F. oven for about 15 minutes.

18. Filo can be used to dress up any of your favorite casserole dishes by simply adding buttered layers of filo on top, then baking as usual.

STORING AND FREEZING FILO

Before Stuffing

1. If your filo has already been frozen once and allowed to defrost, don't put it in the freezer a second time. Be sure to ask the store clerk whether it was received frozen or unfrozen from the distributor. You can, however, transport the filo from the store freezer to your own freezer.

2. To defrost the filo, place it directly into your refrigerator for 1 or 2 days. This way the sheets will separate easily and stay dry. Do not defrost it at room temperature or the sheets will stick together.

3. Filo will keep in the refrigerator 3 to 4 weeks if the package is unopened.

4. Once the package has been opened, it will keep for about 2 weeks if properly sealed. Store it in an airtight plastic bag, pressing out all the air.

After Stuffing

1. You may prepare and stuff the pastry and store it in the refrigerator 2 to 3 days before baking. It can go straight from the refrigerator to the oven.

2. Most filo pastries in this book can be frozen before they are baked or deep-fried. If you are freezing the pastry in a baking pan, be sure to seal it well so that no air gets in. When freezing the small individual shapes, such as the triangles or short rolls, first place them uncovered on a baking sheet in a single layer in the freezer. When they become hard, stack them in a freezer container, separating each layer with a sheet of waxed paper. Cover container tightly. They can be frozen after they are baked as well, but in my opinion the pastries taste better if frozen unbaked.

3. Remove from the freezer about 30 minutes to 1 hour (depending on size of pastry) before baking. Bake frozen pastries a little longer than the time specified in recipe. Also, brush a little extra butter or oil on the pastry while it is baking.

NOTES ON INGREDIENTS

ALMOND PASTE. To make your own, see the instructions included in the recipe for Mhannsha on page 134. If you prefer to use prepared almond paste, make sure the can or package reads "almond paste" and not "almond filling." Substituting one for the other doesn't work.

FETA. Feta, the most popular cheese in Greece, is a crumbly, salty and rather soft white cheese made from sheep's (and sometimes goat's) milk. It is used in Greek salads, in various filo pastries such as *tiropetes* and *spanakopita,* or served simply as an appetizer with olives and bread. You can find it in Greek and Middle Eastern groceries as well as in fine cheese shops. Most important, you should be sure that it is properly stored in the shop where you buy it — it should be immersed in a salty brine to preserve its freshness. Otherwise, it rapidly dries out and develops an unpleasant taste. Some supermarkets sell it prepackaged, but avoid this if possible.

Though feta is a Greek cheese, it is popular all over the world and a wide variety of fetas is available, each with different quali-ties: *Bulgarian* is generally considered to be the creamiest and the best; *Danish,* the most widely distributed in the United States, is made from cow's milk and usually has a milder flavor; *Greek* is wonderfully pungent and sometimes quite salty; *Israeli* is often good but of variable quality; *Romanian* is drier and less expensive than the Bulgarian or Greek fetas; and *domestic* is made from cow's milk and generally has a less interesting flavor than the imported sheep's milk fetas.

No matter which type of feta you buy, expect the flavor to vary; one time it will be pungent and quite salty, another time mild and less salty. The best quality fetas are shipped in large wooden barrels, while those of lesser quality come in large cans.

Whenever you use feta in any filling, omit the salt until *after* you have added the feta. Then, taste the filling and salt accordingly.

GRUYERE. Gruyère, a Swiss or French cheese with a mildly salty and nutty flavor, is most commonly used in French cooking. Amber-colored with small holes, it is similar to "Swiss" cheese but has a much fuller flavor.

HARISSA SAUCE. *Harissa* sauce is a spicy, hot sauce made from chiles, vegetables, oil, garlic, coriander, caraway, salt, cornstarch and citric acid. You may substitute cayenne pepper or Tabasco sauce, as well as an Indonesian Sambal.

HONEY. Some of the pastries in this book use honey syrups. To give a characteristic flavor to your syrup, experiment by using different flavored honeys. Try wildflower or, for a darker, stronger honey flavor, use the famous thyme-scented honey from Mount Hymettus in Greece.

KEFALOTIRI. *Kefalotiri,* a hard, salty, light-yellow grating cheese made from sheep's or goat's milk, is used in pasta dishes and pitas. Sometimes grilled or fried, it is served with bread as an appetizer.

MIZITHRA. *Mizithra* is a mild, lightly salted cheese made with either sheep's or goat's milk. It can be used as a table cheese or as a semi-hard grating cheese for pasta or for stuffing vegetables and meat pies. *Hlori mizithra,* a semi-soft moist cheese, is usually available only in Greece; you can, however, use an Italian semi-dry ricotta (available in the United States) as a substitute.

OLIVE OIL. Olive oil is used predominantly in Mediterranean cooking. For the recipes in this book, a light, fruity olive oil is best. I prefer Greek olive oil, but there are many brands imported to the United States from Spain and Italy that are equally good. California also produces good olive oil. The flavor of olive oil, like wine, is influenced by the soil in which the olive trees grow. You should experiment to find the oil you like best. Check Italian and Middle Eastern markets for the best selection. It's less expensive to buy it by the gallon and share with friends. Or, transfer it into smaller bottles, tightly seal them and store them in a cool, dark place so the oil will not turn rancid.

Virgin olive oil refers to the oil extracted from the first pressing of the olives. The very expensive extra-virgin olive oils from California, France or Tuscany need not be used for the recipes in this book — they are best used to dress salads and to season other foods, such as fresh mozzarella, where the oil's superb flavor can be tasted undistracted by other competing flavors.

ORANGE BLOSSOM WATER. Orange blossom water, also called orange flower water, is made from orange blossoms distilled in water and is used throughout North Africa and in parts of the Middle East to scent and flavor cakes, pastries and dried and fresh fruit compotes.

PARMESAN CHEESE. The dry tasteless powder often packaged as "Parmesan Cheese" has very little in common with *Parmigiano Reggiano,* the most regal of Italian grating cheeses. This cheese, produced in the Emilia region of Italy, is subject to regulations on aging and *is* expensive; but you will find just a little freshly grated Parmesan gives far more flavor to your food than a whole handful of packaged grated Parmesan. Many cheese shops also sell their own freshly grated Parmesan cheese.

A number of less expensive, yet delicious, grating cheeses, which can be substituted for Parmesan, are also available. Among them are *Romano, pecorino, grana sarda* or the very good domestic *Asiago.*

ROSE WATER. Rose water, made from the petals of sweet-smelling roses distilled in water, is used throughout the Arab world and the Middle East to flavor sweet puddings, various nut pastries and fruit compotes.

SAFFRON. Saffron, made from the dried stigma of the *crocus sativus* (a purple-flowered species grown in the Mediterranean region), is both very expensive and rare. There is no substitute for its unique flavor and aroma. Some old filo recipes require an egg wash stained with a touch of saffron to give the top layer a deep yellow-orange hue.

MAKING COMMERCIAL FILO

Filo is usually made commercially from a dough of high-gluten flour, water and salt. Though commercial filo is made by various methods, today the most common is the machine-made employed by large filo companies. But it is still possible to find commercial filo made by hand. One of the more common hand methods is the "stretching" method, which was shown to me by Mr. Migirdich Sagatelyan of San Francisco's Sheherazade Bakery. Mr. Sagatelyan, an Armenian who learned the skill from his father, has been making filo commercially for fifty years. Traditionally, this craft is passed down from father to son. Mr. Sagatelyan claims that it is "a hard, time-consuming job and not profitable to do by hand." As a result, there are few who do it today in this country and even fewer who are willing to learn. He predicts that in twenty to thirty years filo will be made exclusively by machine.

Mr. Sagatelyan's "stretching" method involves mixing together high-gluten flour, water and salt to form a dough. He then divides it into many balls, covers them with a damp towel and leaves them to rest for an hour. Then he rolls out each ball to a flat disk about 14 inches in diameter, sprinkles it with cornstarch and stacks the disks one on top of the other. Just before he's ready to stretch the dough, he rolls out each piece of dough a little bit more until they all measure about 24 inches in diameter. Holding the dough over their hands, he and his brother Mihran begin stretching the dough together with such graceful ease and skill it looks easy. In about 2 minutes the dough is completely stretched and is flung over a large table. Then cornstarch is generously sprinkled and brushed over the sheet of filo. After several sheets of filo have been made in this manner, they are covered with a large canvas sheet. When the process is complete, the filo is cut into rectangular sheets measuring about 12½ inches by 20½ inches. It comes in 1-pound packages, with about 18 to 20 sheets. To make 100 pounds of filo, it takes Mr. Sagatelyan and his brother 9 to 10 hours.

Another method is the "rolling pin" method. Used mostly in Turkey and Syria, it is also fascinating to watch. George Stoyanof of Stoyanof's Cafe and Restaurant in San Francisco uses this method. From Istanbul, of a Greek/Bulgarian background, Mr. Stoyanof makes his filo by combining flour, salt, water, eggs and a tiny bit of olive oil. The eggs make this filo more flavorful. After the dough is mixed, it is kneaded quite a bit and left to stand for an hour. It is then shaped into several balls and left to stand another hour at room temperature. Next, the balls are rolled out a little, sprinkled with cornstarch, stacked, wrapped in plastic wrap and left to stand one day at room temperature. (If the room temperature is more than moderately warm, they are placed in the refrigerator.) When the 20 layers are ready to be rolled out the next day, each layer is generously sprinkled with cornstarch. They are rolled out all together, one on top of the other, with the rolling pin. Then they are turned over and rolled again, wrapped around the rolling pin, and then rolled out again. He repeats this process again and again, constantly working the dough and rolling it so that each time it is larger and thinner. Mr. Stoyanof does this effortlessly, without any of the layers sticking together. He emphatically states, however, that you cannot use this method in your own home. Mr. Stoyanof loves what he does and makes it seem like child's play. To eat filo pastries in a restaurant where the filo is made by hand is a rare pleasure, and it is reflected in the pride Mr. Stoyanof exhibits toward his culinary creations.

Filo can also be made at home. This is referred to as *spitiko* filo by the Greeks, meaning "home filo." Usually it is enriched with a few more ingredients, such as eggs, olive oil or vinegar.

HOMEMADE FILO

The "stretching method" described below is the easiest for making filo at home. To make approximately 1 pound of filo, allow at least 2 hours of work time, especially for your first attempt. Of the various home recipes and methods I've seen, I feel that pastry chef Diane Dexter's is the best and easiest to follow. Here is my version of her recipe.

A Few Tips Before You Begin

1. Avoid making filo in rainy, humid weather — it will be difficult to work with and will take a long time to dry.

2. Use high quality unbleached flour. You'll discover that different commercial flours give slightly different results.

3. You'll need a large work table situated where you can work from all sides. The table should be covered with a clean, smooth tablecloth or sheet.

4. Before you begin stretching the dough, remove all jewelry from your hands to prevent snagging or tearing of the filo.

INGREDIENTS

> 2–2½ cups all-purpose unbleached flour*
>
> 1 large egg, room temperature
>
> ½ cup lukewarm water
>
> ¼ teaspoon salt
>
> 1½ tablespoons light olive oil
>
> ½ teaspoon white vinegar

* This measurement can never be exact since it depends on the type of flour you use and the degree of humidity in the air.

TO ASSEMBLE

Place the flour in a medium-sized bowl. Mix together in a small bowl the egg, water, salt, oil and vinegar. When it is well-mixed, add to the flour and quickly work the dough with your hands, kneading it. Add more flour as needed, until the dough no longer sticks to your hands or the bowl. (Be careful not to add too much flour, or your dough will become stiff and lose its suppleness.) Continue kneading the dough until it is smooth and elastic, about 10 minutes. Cut the dough in half and shape it into 2 smooth balls. Knead again lightly. Flatten each ball slightly, brush with a little oil and place on an oiled plate. Cover with plastic wrap and set in a warm place to rest for 30 to 45 minutes.

Cover your work table with a clean cloth and sprinkle the entire surface with flour. Very gently transfer one of the balls of dough to the center of the table, being careful not to disturb its shape or to make any creases or folds in it. Sprinkle the dough lightly with more flour. With a rolling pin, roll it out *evenly* to about 16 inches in diameter.

Now carefully pick up the dough and place it on the back of your hands (palms down, hands slightly closed and elbows pointed downward). With the dough resting

on your knuckles, begin to stretch it by lifting and turning. As you repeat this continuous motion slowly and evenly, the dough will stretch under its own weight each time you lift and turn.

When the dough becomes too thin and fragile to work in this manner without tearing, lay it over the center of the table and begin stretching it slowly and gently with your fingers, moving around the table as you stretch (never stretch the dough in one place for too long). Continue stretching the dough until it is thin enough to read through, evening out any thick spots. When the dough has been stretched to its limit, trim the thick edges with a sharp knife or scissors. (These scraps can be used again for stretching more dough.) Let the filo dry a little (if it hasn't already) until it feels smooth and satiny, usually 10 to 15 minutes. You can help it along by picking up the dough and fanning it gently. Then, cut the filo into the rectangles or squares needed for your recipe.

If you're not using the filo immediately, stack the sheets, sprinkling generous amounts of cornstarch or semolina between each sheet to prevent them from sticking together. Cover tightly with plastic wrap and refrigerate or freeze.

Repeat this process with the remaining dough.

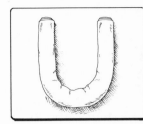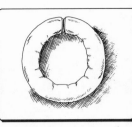

PART TWO

SHAPES

TRIANGLE

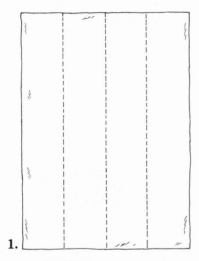

1.

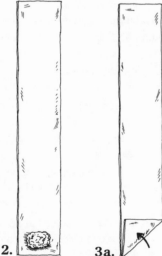

2.

3a.

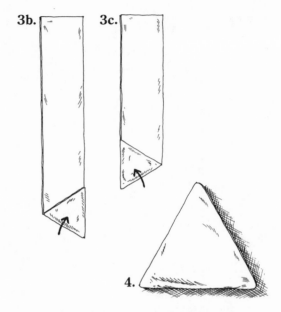

3b. 3c.

4.

1. Cut the filo lengthwise into 4 long strips. Stack the strips and cover them with clear plastic wrap or a slightly damp cloth.

2. Take 2 strips from the stack and lay them out one on top of the other. Lightly brush the top strip with butter or oil. Place about 1 tablespoon of filling at bottom of strip.

3a, b, c. Fold one corner of filo over the filling, alternating from left to right until you reach the midway point. Brush the pastry again with a little butter or oil. Continue folding to the end.

4. Place the triangle seam side down on a greased baking sheet. Brush top with more butter or oil.

SHORT ROLL

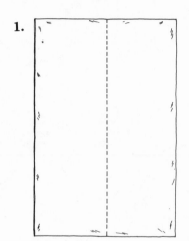

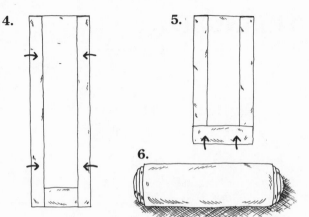

1. Cut filo lengthwise into 2 strips. Stack the strips and cover with clear plastic wrap or a slightly damp cloth.

2. For each pastry roll, take 2 strips from the stack and lay them out one on top of the other. Brush the top strip with butter or oil. Place about 4 tablespoons of filling at the bottom of the strip.

3. Fold the bottom edge of the filo over filling.

4. Fold left edge of the filo strip over about ½ inch. Brush folded edge with a little butter or oil. Repeat the process with the right edge of the filo strip.

5. Roll up the pastry, stopping halfway through to brush the top with a little more butter or oil. Then continue rolling pastry to the end.

6. Place the roll seam side down on a lightly greased baking sheet. Brush the top of the pastry with butter or oil.

DOUBLE ROLL

4.

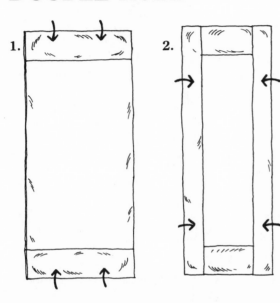

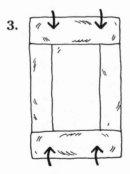

1. Cut filo lengthwise into 2 strips. Stack the strips and cover with clear plastic wrap or a slightly damp cloth. For each pastry, take 2 strips from the stack and lay them out one on top of the other. Brush the top strip with butter or oil. Place about 4 tablespoons of filling at the bottom of the strip and 4 tablespoons at the top of the strip. Fold the bottom edge of the filo over filling. Repeat the fold with the top edge.

2. Fold the left edge of the filo strip over about ¾ inch. Brush the folded edge with a little butter or oil. Repeat the process with the right edge of the filo strip.

3. Roll the bottom of the pastry toward the center. Repeat with the top, until both rolls meet at the center.

4. Place the roll, on a lightly greased baking sheet. Brush the top of the pastry with butter or oil.

BOAT

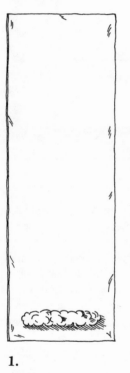

1.

2.

1. Cut filo lengthwise into 4½-inch-wide strips. Stack the strips and cover with clear plastic wrap or a slightly damp cloth. For each boat, take 2 strips from the stack and lay them out one on top of the other. Lightly brush the top strip with butter or oil. Place about 2 tablespoons of filling at the bottom of the strip.

2. Fold the bottom edge of the filo strip over the filling. Next, fold the left edge of the filo strip over about ½ inch. Repeat the fold on the right edge. Brush both folded edges with butter or oil. Before rolling up this pastry, lay out 2 more strips of filo and place at an angle at the top edge of the filled strip, as shown in the drawing. Place 2 tablespoons of filling at the bottom of the strip and continue as for the first strip.

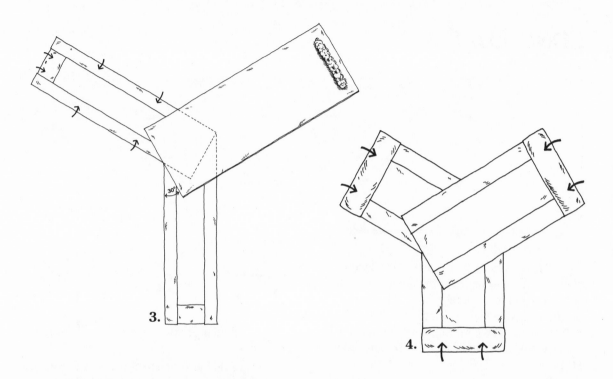

3. Lay out the final 2 strips and place at an angle on top of both filled strips. Place 2 tablespoons of filling at the bottom of the strip and continue as for the first 2 strips.

4. One at a time, roll all 3 of the filled strips toward the center to form a triangle, stopping halfway to brush the top of the pastry with a little butter or oil.

5. Place the garnish of your choice in the center of the boat. Brush the top with a little more butter or oil.

LONG ROLL

1.

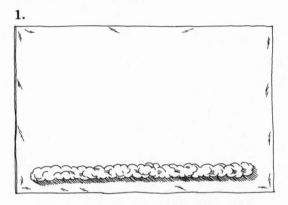

1. On a clean flat surface, place 2 whole sheets of filo, one on top of the other. Cover the filo you're not immediately using with clear plastic wrap or a slightly damp cloth. Brush the entire surface of the top sheet with butter or oil. Place 1 to 1½ cups of filling at the bottom of the strip.

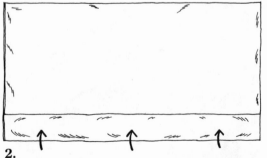

2.

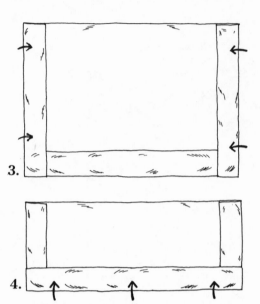

2. Fold the bottom edge of the filo over the filling.

3. Fold the left edge of the filo sheet over about 2 inches, then brush the folded edge with a little butter or oil. Repeat the process with the right edge of the filo sheet.

4. Roll up the pastry, stopping halfway to brush the top generously with butter or oil. Then continue rolling pastry to the end.

5. Place the roll seam side down on a lightly greased baking sheet. Brush the top of the pastry with butter or oil.

5.

Now that you know how to make the long roll, you can use it to make a variety of attractive shapes. I'll show you how to make the small spiral and give you some ideas for other kinds of shapes.

SMALL SPIRAL

    1. Follow instructions for the Long Roll shape on page 36.

    2. Roll the pastry tightly to form a spiral shape.

1.

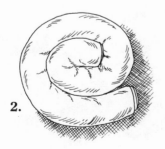

2.

OTHER SHAPES BASED ON THE LONG ROLL

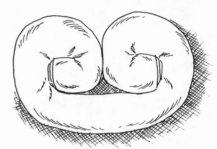

DOUBLE SPIRAL

BUTTERFLY

FIGURE EIGHT

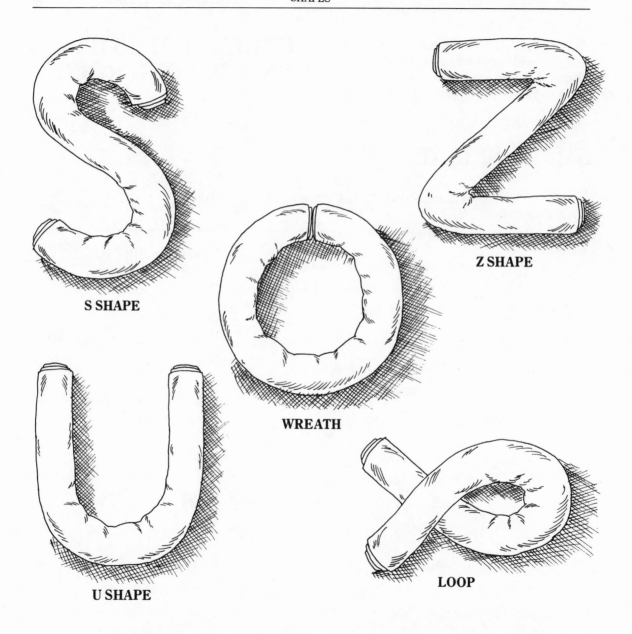

S SHAPE

WREATH

Z SHAPE

U SHAPE

LOOP

LARGE SPIRAL

1. On a clean flat surface, place 3 whole sheets of filo, one on top of the other, brushing each sheet with a little butter or oil before adding the next. Cover the filo you're not immediately using with clear plastic wrap or a slightly damp cloth. Overlap one end of the filo about 2 inches with 3 more whole sheets, one on top of the other as before. Then repeat with a third set of filo sheets, overlapping one end of the second set about 2 inches.

Place 3 to 4 cups of filling at the bottom of the strip.

2. Fold the bottom edge of the filo over the filling.

3. Fold the left edge of the filo over about 2 inches. Brush the folded edge with a little butter or oil. Repeat the process with the right edge of the filo.

4. Carefully roll up the pastry, stopping halfway to brush the top generously with butter or oil. Then continue rolling up pastry to the end.

5. Turn the pastry until it lies seam side down and loosely roll it to form a spiral shape.

6. With 2 wide spatulas, carefully pick up the pastry and place it seam side down on a lightly greased baking sheet. Brush the top of the pastry generously with butter or oil. (If you wish, sprinkle sesame or poppy seeds on top.)

Note: To make an even longer and more spectacular spiral, you can simply extend the coil by adding one or more segments.

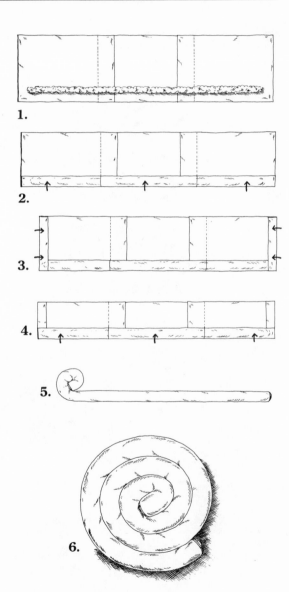

ROLLED SPIRAL

1.

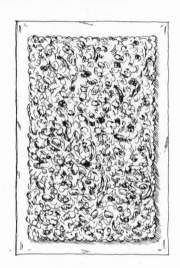

4.

2.

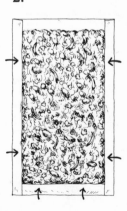

3.

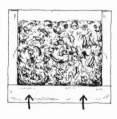

1. Place 1 whole sheet of filo on a clean flat surface. Cover the filo that is not being immediately used with a slightly damp cloth or clear plastic wrap. Brush the entire surface with butter or oil. Sprinkle a thin layer of very fine bread crumbs over the surface of the filo. Then cover with another layer of filo. Repeat this process until you have 4 or 5 layers of filo and bread crumbs.

Spread the filling over the entire surface of the filo. (If you're making 2 rolls, remember to use only half of your filling.)

2. Fold the bottom edge of the filo over the filling. Brush with butter or oil.

Fold the left edge of the filo sheet over about 1½ inches. Brush the folded edge with a little more butter or oil. Repeat the process with the right edge of the filo sheet.

3. Roll up the pastry, stopping halfway to brush the top generously with butter or oil. Then continue rolling pastry to the end.

4. Place the spiral seam side down on a lightly greased baking sheet. Brush the top of the pastry with butter or oil.

ZIGZAG

1.

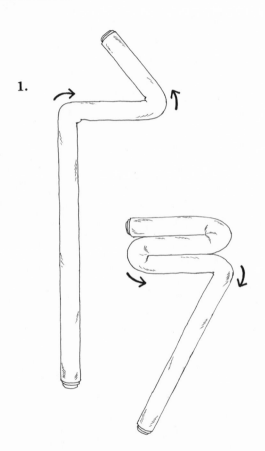

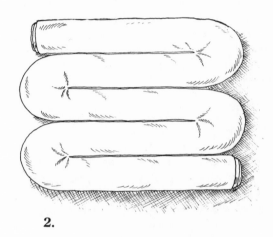

2.

Follow instructions for the long roll shape on
page 36, (or, if you prefer to make a larger
pastry, follow the first 4 steps of instructions for
the large spiral shape on page 39).

    1. Turn the pastry so that it lies seam side
down and carefully shape the pastry to form a
zig zag by bending it as shown.

    2. With a wide spatula, carefully pick up
the pastry and place it seam side down on a
lightly greased baking sheet. Brush the top
of the pastry with butter or oil.

INDIVIDUAL WRAP

Although I have not included any recipes for this shape in the book, you can make easy, attractive hors d'oeuvres by wrapping your favorite cooked sausages or various semi-cooked vegetables, such as asparagus, served with a tasty sauce.

1. Cut filo lengthwise into 2 or 3 strips (depending on size of the food to be wrapped). Stack strips and cover with clear plastic wrap or a slightly damp cloth. Lay out one strip of filo and lightly brush it with butter or oil. Place an asparagus spear or a small cooked sausage at the bottom edge of the strip, with its tip extending slightly over the edge of the filo.

Fold the bottom edge of filo over the vegetable or sausage. Brush with a little butter or oil.

2. Fold the left edge of the filo strip over about ½ inch. Brush the folded edge lightly with butter or oil.

3. Roll it up, stopping halfway to brush the top with a little butter or oil. Then continue rolling the pastry to the end.

Place the pastry seam side down on a lightly greased baking sheet. Brush the top of the rolled pastry with a little more butter or oil.

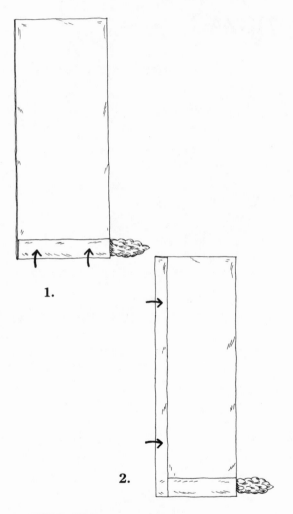

1.

2.

3.

BALL

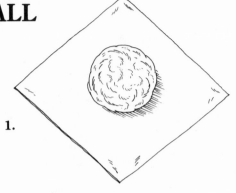

1.

2.

3.

4.

1. Cut filo into 5-inch-square pieces. Stack the pieces and cover with clear plastic wrap or a slightly damp cloth. For each ball, lay out 3 squares of filo, one on top of the other. Lightly brush each square with butter or oil. Place 1 meatball (or other filling) in the center of the square.

2. Fold 1 corner of the filo over the filling.

3. Continue folding over the rest of the corners, brushing with a little butter or oil after each fold so it will seal better.

4. Brush entire ball with butter or oil. Place each ball seam side down on a greased baking sheet, unless you are deep-frying them.

SOUFFLE

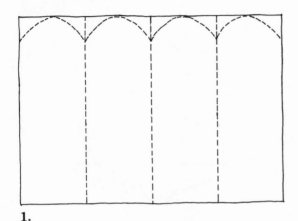

1.

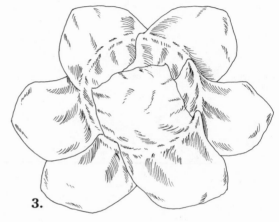

3.

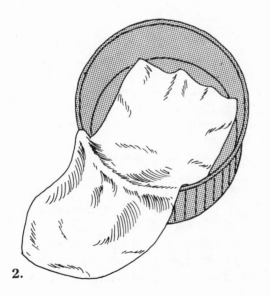

2.

Because soufflé is such a delicate mixture, it is important to assemble the filo as quickly as possible.

1. Cut 2 whole filo sheets crosswise into 4 petal shapes, as shown. Stack the petal-shaped strips and cover with clear plastic wrap or a slightly damp cloth.

2. Grease a 1½- or 2-quart soufflé dish. Lay out 1 strip of filo, brush it with butter or oil and lay half of it in the soufflé dish with the rounded end hanging over the edge.

3. Continue overlapping the petal-shaped strips in this manner, brushing each with butter or oil, until you have covered the entire soufflé dish.

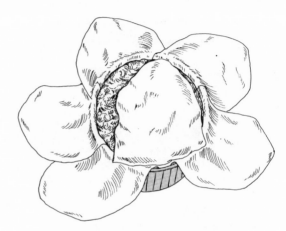

4.

4. Pour in soufflé mixture and begin folding the petal-shaped strips *loosely* up and over the filling, so that the soufflé has room to rise.

5. Brush the top with butter or oil.

For variation: You may use individual small soufflé dishes or muffin tins. Be sure to grease each container generously. Simply cut filo into proportionately smaller pieces to line the individual soufflé dish. For the muffin tins, use 4 layers of filo strips cut to appropriate size. The filo should extend ½ inch or so over the top edge of the tins. Fill the tins ¾ full. Fold the extending edges of the filo over and tuck them neatly against the sides of the tins.

5.

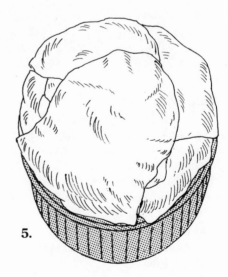

SQUARE OR RECTANGULAR PAN

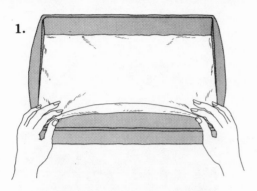

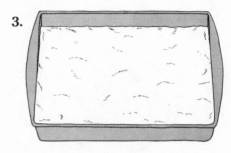

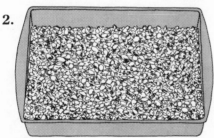

For Baklava Recipes

1. Brush the bottom and sides of the baking pan with melted butter. Cut filo sheets to fit the pan. Stack sheets and cover with clear plastic wrap or a slightly damp cloth. Lay out 1 cut sheet of filo at the bottom of the pan and brush evenly with butter. Now lay down 3 more sheets, brushing each lightly with butter before laying the next on top.

2. Spread a thin layer of nut mixture evenly over the filo.

3. Continue the layering process in this manner: after every fourth sheet of filo, spread a thin layer of nut mixture. After the final layer of nuts has been spread, continue layering with 10 to 15 more filo sheets (remembering to brush each with butter). The more layers of filo on top that you use, the higher and more elegant your pastry.

4. Before baking, use a sharp knife to cut the pastry into square- or diamond-shaped pieces, cutting only halfway through the pastry.

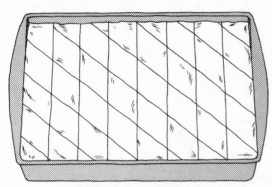

Diamond-cut baklava

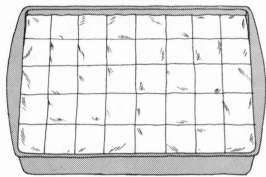

Square-cut baklava

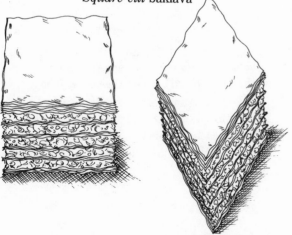

For All Other Recipes

(Numbers refer to the illustrations on preceding page.)

1. Brush the bottom and sides of the baking pan with melted butter or oil. Cut filo sheets to fit the pan. Stack sheets and cover with clear plastic wrap or a slightly damp cloth. Lay out 1 cut sheet of filo at the bottom of the pan and brush evenly with butter or oil. Now lay down 7 to 8 more sheets, brushing each lightly with butter or oil before laying the next sheet on top.

2. Spread the filling evenly over the layered filo.

3. Cover the filling with 8 to 10 more sheets of filo, brushing each lightly with butter or oil. Important note: *do not pre-cut* pastry before baking, because the filling might ooze out into the top layer of filo, especially if it is a more liquid filling.

RING MOLD

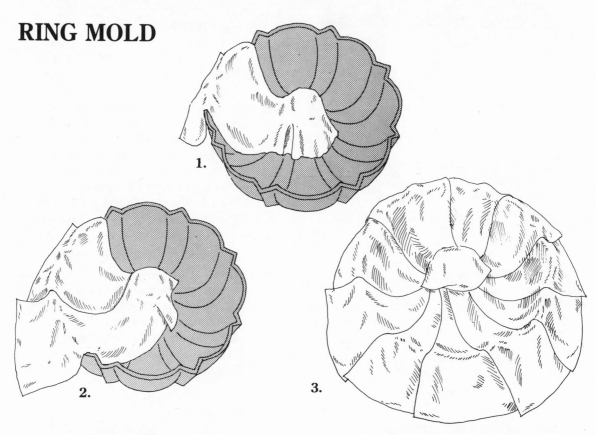

1.

2.

3.

1. Take 10 whole sheets of filo and cut lengthwise in thirds. Stack the strips and cover with clear plastic wrap or a slightly damp cloth.

Grease a large (10-inch-diameter) bundt pan. (**For variation:** any type of molded baking pan will work well with filo.) Take 1 strip of the cut filo, brush it with butter or oil and gently drape it into the pan, letting the middle of the filo

hang down in a "U" shape. One end of the filo should fall over the outer edge of the pan and the other end should lay over the center tube.

2. Continue draping strips brushed with butter or oil all the way around the pan, overlapping each by ½ inch as it is put in the pan.

3. Here's how it looks before the filling is added.

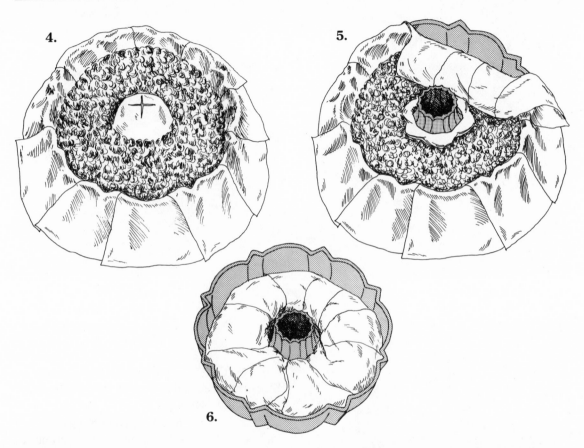

4. Pour in the filling. With a sharp knife, cut a + through the filo covering the center tube.

5. Now fold the cut ends away from the center tube down over the filling. Brush with butter or oil. Fold the overhanging ends from the outer rim of pan over the filling.

6. Be sure to tuck edges under so that the pastry lays flat. Brush the top again with butter or oil.

After the pastry has baked, let it rest about 10 minutes before unmolding, then turn it onto a flat baking sheet and place it back in a 400°F. oven about 5 minutes or until the filo gets crisp again.

SIMPLE ROUND

1.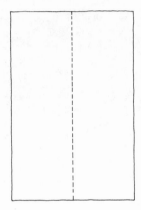

3.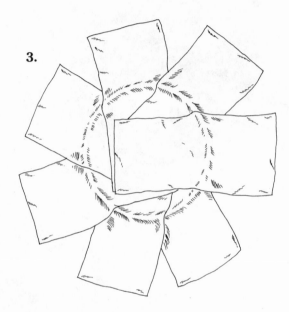

2.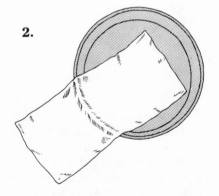

1. Cut filo lengthwise into 2 long strips. Stack the strips and cover with clear plastic wrap or a slightly damp cloth.

2. Brush a round, shallow baking dish (9 inches or 9½ inches) with butter or oil. Lay out 1 strip of filo, with half of it inside the pan and the other half outside the pan. Brush with butter or oil.

3. Continue overlapping strips on top of each other, using 6 or 7 strips to complete the circle.

Note: Each new strip of filo should be brushed with butter or oil after it is put in place.

4.

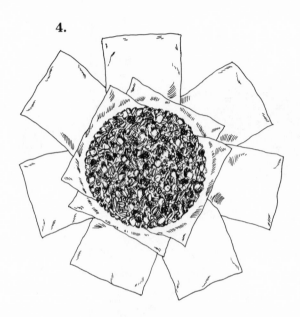

5.

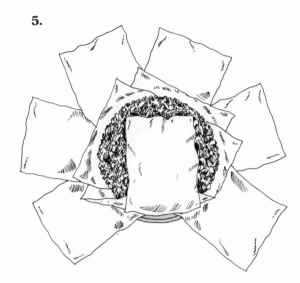

6.

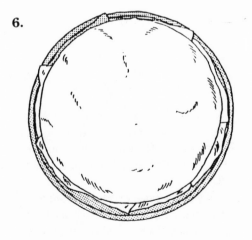

4. Then cut one whole sheet of filo in half crosswise. Lay the 2 pieces, one on top of the other, in the center of the pan. Spread the filling evenly over the filo.

5. Fold the strips up and over toward the center to cover the filling completely.

6. Cut 4 whole sheets of filo in a round shape, the same size as your pan. Lay each round sheet, one on top of the other, over the pastry. Brush each round sheet, and the top, with butter or oil.

ELABORATE ROUND

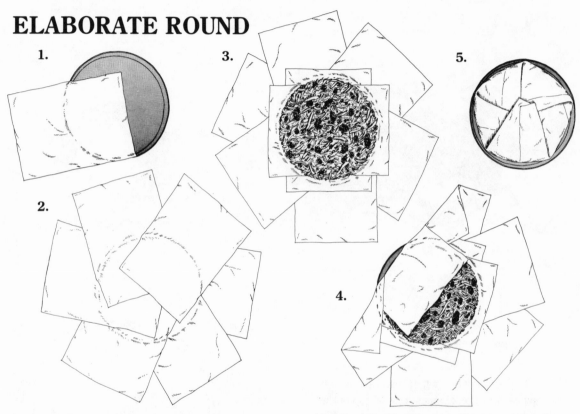

1. Brush a large (14 inch by ¾ inch) pizza pan with butter or oil. Lay out 1 whole sheet of filo, so that half lays inside of the pan and the other half lays outside of the pan. Brush with butter or oil.

2. Continue overlapping sheets on top of each other, using 6 sheets to complete the circle.

Note: Each new sheet of filo should be brushed with butter or oil after it is put in place.

3. Lay 4 more sheets, one on top of the other, in the center of the pan (alternating each sheet horizontally and vertically). Spread filling evenly in the pan.

4. Fold sheets toward the center to cover the filling completely.

5. Filling is now covered completely.

6.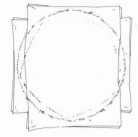

7.

8.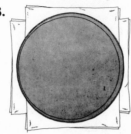

9.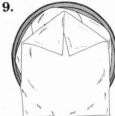

10.

6. Lay 3 more sheets, one on top of the other, over the pastry (alternating each sheet horizontally and vertically). Now lay a large, flat baking sheet over the pastry and quickly flip the pastry onto the baking sheet.

7. Remove the pizza pan. Bring the edges of the filo sheets over the pastry.

8. Lay 3 more sheets on top of this, again alternating each sheet horizontally and vertically. Place the pizza pan back on top of the pastry and flip it once more.

9. Remove the baking sheet. Bring all the edges of the filo over the pastry. (It will look much like the package shown in drawing 5.) Place 1 sheet of filo on top of the pastry. Fold the right-hand corner up and over, then the left-hand corner, continuing until all 4 corners are folded up and over.

10. Repeat with each sheet of filo remaining in your 1-pound package until they have all been used.

CREATE YOUR OWN SHAPE

A Few Guidelines To Remember

1. Always use at least 2 sheets of filo, one on top of the other. Remember to butter or oil the filo before adding filling.

2. Try not to overstuff your pastry, or the filling will leak out. Your filling should not be too liquid.

3. Work as quickly as possible. Cover the unused filo with plastic wrap or a slightly damp cloth.

4. If you have created an unusually intricate or delicate shape, be sure to seal the edges of the filo with a little beaten egg, so that it won't break open while it is baked or deep-fried.

5. For a rich golden color, brush the top of your pastries with a little beaten egg yolk.

6. If your shape is small, baking time will vary from 15 to 25 minutes. Remember to let your pastries bake until they are golden brown. If you have created a large shape, adjust your baking time accordingly, anywhere from 30 minutes to 1 hour.

7. For variety, you may sprinkle sesame or poppy seeds, paprika or any edible decoration on top of your pastry. Desserts can be dipped or covered with chocolate, powdered sugar or finely chopped nuts, such as pistachios.

8. A few shapes you may want to explore: free-form shapes, cut out with scissors, such as a fish, a heart or a flower; shapes from *origami*, the Japanese art of paper-folding.

NOTES FOR YOUR OWN SHAPES

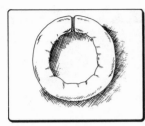

PART THREE

RECIPES

Cheese

BLINTZES
JEWISH

For an elegant yet easy to prepare breakfast or brunch, serve these blintzes with a platter of fresh fruit. Many of my friends like this better than the traditional version.

SHAPE   Short Roll or Double Roll
(page 32 or 33)

FILO   About ½ pound

FOR BRUSHING FILO   Butter, melted

FILLING

  2 cups ricotta cheese (*or* farmer's *or* pot cheese)

  1 egg

  Pinch of salt

  1 tablespoon sugar

  1 tablespoon melted butter

  1 teaspoon freshly squeezed lemon juice

GARNISH

  Sour cream and strawberry jam or applesauce

TO ASSEMBLE

Mix together all of the above filling ingredients. Beat with an electric mixer or with a heavy wooden spoon until smooth.

Follow the folding instructions for the shape you have chosen on page 32 or 33.

Bake on a greased baking sheet in a preheated 375° F. oven until golden brown, about 20 minutes. Serve immediately, garnished with dollops of sour cream and strawberry jam or applesauce.

These are wonderful when they're cold, too, but they won't look as attractive as the first day they're made.

Serves 5 as a brunch entrée.

TIROPETES
GREEK

A bowl of *Kalamata* olives and a platter of these golden crispy filo triangles stuffed with cheese makes one of the most satisfying appetizers in the world. If you like a stronger and saltier flavor, use a larger proportion of feta (or use only feta) when making the filling. For parties you can make *tiropetes* well in advance and freeze them before baking.

SHAPE   Triangle (page 31)

FILO   About ½ pound

FOR BRUSHING FILO   Butter, melted

FILLING

    ½ pint cottage cheese

    ½ pound feta cheese

    3 eggs, beaten

    ¼ teaspoon dried dill weed
      or ½ teaspoon fresh dill weed

    1 tablespoon chopped fresh chives

    2 teaspoons finely chopped fresh
      parsley

TO ASSEMBLE

In a bowl, crumble the feta cheese with your fingers or a fork. Add the rest of the ingredients and mix well.

Follow the folding instructions on page 31.

Bake on a greased baking sheet in a preheated 375° F. oven until golden brown, about 20 minutes. Cool a few minutes before serving.

Makes about 20 triangles.

SAGANAKI
GREEK

This idea is adapted to filo from the *Saganaki* dish in which *kefalotiri* cheese is grilled or fried and served sprinkled with a bit of lemon juice. It is very popular in Greek cafés where it is brought to the table very hot, then doused with heated brandy and ignited for a dramatic presentation. Lemon juice is squeezed over the top to put out the flame, and then it is served with fresh bread.

SHAPE   Triangle or Short Roll
    (page 31 or 32)

FILO   About ½ pound

FOR BRUSHING FILO
    Unsalted butter, melted

FILLING
    ½ pound *kefalotiri* cheese, cut into
        1½-inch squares that are ¼-inch
        thick
    1 lemon, for squeezing over the top

TO ASSEMBLE

After you have cut the *kefalotiri* into 1½-inch square pieces, follow the folding instructions for the shape you have chosen on page 31 or 32.

    Bake in a 375° F. oven until golden brown, about 25 minutes. Serve directly from the oven with a squeeze of lemon juice over the top. It's important to serve these filo pastries immediately, since the cheese becomes hard and rubbery when it cools.

Makes about 16 pastries.

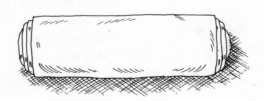

BOUGATSA
GREEK

This is a Cretan specialty, delicious when purchased in the early morning from one of the island's small local bakeries and eaten while still warm from the oven. In Crete, it is made with fresh *mizithra* cheese, but since fresh *mizithra* is not usually available here, I use the more common semi-soft *mizithra* or Italian semi-dry ricotta cheese mixed with other, milder cheeses. It is perfect for a champagne brunch!

SHAPE   Short Roll or Large Spiral
     (page 32 or 39)

FILO   About ¾ pound for short roll;
     ½ pound for large spiral

FOR BRUSHING FILO
     Unsalted butter, melted

FILLING
     ½ pound semi-soft *mizithra* cheese *or*
     Italian semi-dry ricotta cheese,
     crumbled
     ½ pound cottage cheese
     ½ pound ricotta cheese
     4 ounces cream cheese, room
     temperature
     1 tablespoon sugar
     ⅛ teaspoon freshly grated nutmeg

TOPPING
     Powdered sugar

TO ASSEMBLE

Crumble the *mizithra* (or Italian semi-dry ricotta) with a fork or your hands. Mix in the cottage cheese, ricotta, cream cheese, sugar and nutmeg. In an electric mixer, beat everything until it is light and well-mixed.

Follow the folding instructions for the shape you have chosen on page 32 or 39, but if you are using the short roll, make the roll a little flatter than usual so that it looks more like a packet than a roll.

Place the pastries on a greased baking sheet and bake in a 375° F. oven until golden brown, about 25 minutes for the short roll and about 35 to 40 minutes for the large spiral. When you take it out of the oven, sprinkle the top with powdered sugar. Let the pastry cool about 15 minutes before serving.

Serves 6 as a brunch entrée.

CHEESE SOUFFLE
FRENCH

Try making this with any number of savory soufflés, adding fresh garden herbs, lightly cooked fresh vegetables or diced ham or bacon, to your basic cheese soufflé.

SHAPE   Soufflé (page 44)

FILO   About ¼ pound

FOR BRUSHING FILO   Butter, melted

FILLING

    4 tablespoons butter
    ¼ cup flour
    1 cup milk
    ½ cup freshly grated Parmesan cheese
    ¼ teaspoon salt
    Pinch of white pepper
    4 eggs, room temperature, separated

TO ASSEMBLE

Over low heat melt 4 tablespoons butter. Using a wire whisk, blend in the flour, then slowly add the milk, stirring constantly until smooth and thick. Remove from the heat, add the cheese and season with salt and white pepper.

Beat the egg yolks, mix them into the milk mixture and let cool. Then beat the egg whites until stiff. Mix about 2 tablespoons of the egg whites into the milk mixture, then add the rest of the whites all at once and gently fold in.

Follow the folding instructions on page 44.

Bake in a preheated 350° F. oven until golden brown, about 35 to 40 minutes. Serve at once.

Serves 4 as a lunch entrée.

Vegetables

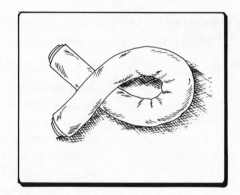

COUNTRY-STYLE MUSHROOMS
FRENCH

It's remarkable how a little garlic and some bacon can heighten the flavor of our somewhat bland cultivated mushrooms. But then, the French do know a trick or two. This dish is even better with fresh wild mushrooms like *cèpes* or *chanterelles*.

SHAPE   Boat, Loop or Wreath
   (page 34, 37 or 38)

FILO   About ¾ pound for boat; ½ pound
   for loop or wreath

FOR BRUSHING FILO   Butter, melted

FILLING

   6 slices bacon

   1 onion, chopped

   3 cloves garlic, minced

   1 pound fresh mushrooms, sliced

   2 teaspoons freshly squeezed lemon
   juice

   Salt and pepper to taste

   2 tablespoons finely chopped fresh
   parsley

   2 tablespoons fine bread crumbs

FOR GARNISHING BOAT SHAPE

   12 whole mushrooms

   Butter

   Parsley sprigs

TO ASSEMBLE

In a skillet, cook the bacon until crisp. Drain, crumble and set aside. In the bacon fat, sauté the onion and garlic until golden. Add the mushrooms and cook about 4 minutes. Add the lemon juice, salt, pepper and parsley. Remove from the heat. Mix in the crumbled bacon and bread crumbs.

Follow the folding instructions for the shape you have chosen on page 34, 37 or 38. Use the whole mushrooms to garnish the center of the boats and dot them with a little butter.

Bake on a greased baking sheet in a preheated 375° F. oven until golden brown, about 25 minutes. Garnish each pastry with parsley sprigs when they come out of the oven.

Makes 6 boats or 4 wreaths or 4 loops.

ZUCCHINI PIE
FRENCH

Throughout the Mediterranean there is a long tradition of *tourtes* or pies made with vegetables and greens, a little local cheese and filo. This is a light French-inspired version, similar to quiche.

SHAPE   Simple Round (page 50)

FILO   About ¼ pound

FOR BRUSHING FILO   Butter, melted

FILLING

    2 eggs, beaten

    1 cup heavy cream

    Salt and white pepper to taste

    ⅛ teaspoon freshly grated nutmeg

    2 medium zucchini, sliced

    ⅔ cup grated Swiss *or* Gruyère cheese

TO ASSEMBLE

In a bowl, mix together all of the ingredients.

Follow the folding instructions on page 50.

Bake in a preheated 350° F. oven for 30 to 35 minutes. Let pie cool for about 30 minutes before cutting.

Serves 4 as a light entrée.

SPANAKOPITA I
GREEK

Spanakopita is one of those classic Greek dishes that you never tire of, no matter how many times you've had it. The slightly earthy taste of the spinach and salty tang of feta with the delicacy of the filo is a fine flavor combination. I make it in several versions, two of which are given here.

SHAPE Square or Rectangular Pan or Triangle (page 46 or 31)

FILO About ½ pound

FOR BRUSHING FILO Olive oil

FILLING

2 pounds fresh spinach with stems removed *or* 2 packages frozen chopped spinach, defrosted

3 tablespoons olive oil

1 bunch green onions, chopped (including the green tops)

½ pound feta cheese

1 bunch fresh parsley, chopped

3 cloves garlic, minced

1½ teaspoons dill weed, fresh if possible

Freshly ground pepper to taste

TO ASSEMBLE

If you are using fresh spinach, wash each leaf and dry thoroughly. If you are using frozen spinach, let it drain thoroughly in a colander, squeezing out the excess moisture.

In a large pot, heat the olive oil. Add the green onions and spinach and cook, stirring constantly until the spinach wilts. This takes just a few minutes. Then place it in a colander, let it drain completely and set aside.

In a separate bowl, crumble the feta cheese with your fingers or a fork. Mix in the parsley, garlic, dill weed and pepper, then add the drained spinach.

Follow the folding instructions for the shape you have chosen on page 46 or 31.

For the square or rectangular shape, bake in a preheated 350° F. oven until golden brown, about 35 minutes. For the triangle shape, bake in a preheated 375° F. oven until golden brown, about 20 minutes.

Serves 6 as a light entrée.

SPANAKOPITA II
GREEK

SHAPE   Square or Rectangular Pan or Triangle (page 46 or 31)

FILO   About ½ pound

FOR BRUSHING FILO   Olive oil

FILLING

   1 pound fresh spinach with stems removed *or* 1 package frozen chopped spinach, defrosted

   4 tablespoons butter

   1 onion, chopped

   Pepper to taste

   ¾ cup feta cheese, crumbled

   3 eggs, beaten

   2 tablespoons flour

   1 cup milk

   Pinch of white pepper

   Pinch of freshly grated nutmeg

TO ASSEMBLE

Prepare the fresh or frozen spinach as in the previous recipe.

In a large pot, melt 2 tablespoons of the butter and sauté the onion until golden. Then add the spinach and cook, stirring constantly, until it wilts. This takes just a few minutes. Then place it in a colander, drain excess liquid and transfer to a large bowl. Add the pepper and the crumbled feta cheese. When the spinach has cooled a bit, mix in the beaten eggs.

In a saucepan, melt the remaining 2 tablespoons of butter. Using a wire whisk, mix in the flour, then add the milk slowly, whisking constantly, until the sauce is smooth and slightly thickened. Remove from the heat and season with white pepper and nutmeg. Combine this white sauce with the spinach mixture.

Follow the folding instructions on page 46 or 31.

For the square or rectangular shape, bake in a preheated 350° F. oven until golden brown, about 30 minutes. For the triangle shape, bake in a preheated 375° F. oven, about 20 minutes.

Serves 4 to 6 as a light entrée.

SWISS CHARD AND MUSHROOM PIE
MEDITERRANEAN

This pie is based on the many *hortopites* or filo pies made with *mizithra* cheese and tender young greens and herbs gathered on the Greek hillsides. Since the fresh Greek *mizithra* is rarely available in the United States, use the Italian semi-dry ricotta or, when you can find it, semi-soft *mizithra*.

SHAPE   Square or Rectangular
   Pan (page 46)

FILO   About ½ pound

FOR BRUSHING FILO   Butter, melted

FILLING
   1 pound Swiss chard
   3 tablespoons olive oil
   1 bunch green onions, chopped
      (including the green tops)
   4 cloves garlic, minced
   ½ pound fresh mushrooms, sliced
   ¼ pound semi-soft *mizithra* cheese *or*
      Italian semi-dry ricotta
   1 pound ricotta cheese
   3 eggs, beaten
   1 teaspoon dried sweet basil
   Pinch of freshly grated nutmeg
   Salt and pepper to taste
   8 thin slices of cooked ham (optional)

TO ASSEMBLE

Wash the Swiss chard well. Discard the tough part of the stalks. Chop up the chard and steam or boil it in a very small amount of water until the stems are tender, about 8 minutes. Place in a colander and drain thoroughly. Set aside.

Heat the olive oil in a large skillet. Sauté the green onions, garlic and mushrooms quickly over high heat, stirring constantly, for about 2 minutes. Add this mixture to the Swiss chard and let all of the liquid drain completely. In a bowl, crumble the *mizithra* with your hands. Mix in the ricotta cheese, eggs, basil, nutmeg, salt and pepper. Add the drained Swiss chard mixture and mix well.

Follow the folding instructions for the shape you have chosen on page 46. Before covering the filling with the top layers of filo, lay the optional ham slices over the entire

Continued on next page

filling. Then continue with the layering process.

Bake in a preheated 375° F. oven until golden brown, about 30 minutes. Let cool 15 minutes before cutting.

Serves 6 as a light entrée.

For variation: In place of the Swiss chard, you may use any other greens such as dandelion or collard greens, spinach, sorrel or a mixture of them. Omit the ham to make a delicious vegetarian entrée.

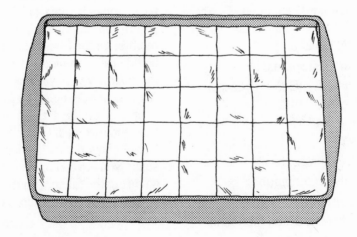

SKORDALIA
GREEK

Only for dedicated garlic lovers, this potent mix of potatoes, olive oil and fresh garlic is traditionally served in Greece as a condiment with a variety of fish, lamb and vegetable dishes. But encased in filo, it becomes a unique addition to your repertoire of appetizers. Its taste is somewhat like a spicy potato knish.

SHAPE   Zigzag (page 41)

FILO   About ¾ pound

FOR BRUSHING FILO   Olive oil

FILLING

   2 pounds potatoes, peeled

   ½ cup water

   ½ cup olive oil

   ¼ cup wine vinegar

   1 head of garlic (10–13 peeled cloves) very finely minced or pureed

   1½ teaspoons salt

   1 egg yolk

TO ASSEMBLE

Steam or boil the potatoes until they are tender, about 30 minutes. Then transfer them to a bowl and mash, adding the water. As you continue to mash the potatoes, slowly add the olive oil and vinegar, alternately. Then mix in the garlic and salt. After the potatoes have cooled a bit, stir in the egg yolk, mixing thoroughly.

Follow the folding instructions on page 41.

Bake on a greased baking sheet in a preheated 350° F. oven until golden brown, about 30 minutes. (These may also be deep-fried.)

Makes 6 pastries.

BEETS WITH GARLIC POTATOES
GREEK

SHAPE   Square or Rectangular Pan (page 46)

FILO   About ½ pound

FOR BRUSHING FILO   Olive oil

FILLING

     4 medium-sized beets

     2 pounds potatoes, peeled

     ½ cup water

     ½ cup olive oil

     ¼ cup wine vinegar

     1½ teaspoons salt

     8–10 cloves garlic, minced

     1 tablespoon capers, drained

     1 tablespoon finely chopped fresh parsley

TOPPING

     Sour cream

     Chives

TO ASSEMBLE

Remove the beet tops. Place the beets in a pan and cover with water. Bring to a boil. Lower flame and simmer until the beets are cooked, about 40 minutes, depending on the size of the beets. Then peel the skins and cut the beets into ¼-inch slices. Set aside.

Steam or boil the potatoes until they are cooked, about 30 minutes. Transfer them to a bowl and mash, adding the water. Continuing to mash the potatoes, slowly add the olive oil and vinegar, alternately. Mix in the salt, garlic, capers and parsley.

Follow the folding instructions for the shape you have chosen on page 46. To layer the filling, first make a layer of beets, then spread half of the garlic potatoes on top of that. Cover with another layer of beets, followed by the remaining garlic potatoes. Continue with the filo layers according to the instructions.

Bake in a preheated 400° F. oven until golden brown, about 35 minutes. Let cool about 20 minutes before serving. Serve with a dollop of sour cream sprinkled with a few chives.

Serves 6 as a side dish or vegetarian entrée.

EGGPLANT WITH MUSHROOMS
ARMENIAN

All the cuisines of the Middle East share a similar range of ingredients and flavors. Eggplant appears in all kinds of guises.

SHAPE   Triangle (page 31)

FILO   About ¾ pound

FOR BRUSHING FILO   Olive oil

FILLING

> 1 medium eggplant, cut in ½-inch cubes
>
> ⅓ cup olive oil
>
> 1 medium onion, chopped
>
> 3 cloves garlic, minced
>
> 1 small zucchini, sliced
>
> 1 8-ounce can tomato sauce
>
> Salt to taste
>
> ¼ teaspoon pepper
>
> ¼ pound fresh mushrooms, sliced

TO ASSEMBLE

Heat the olive oil in a heavy skillet. Add the eggplant, onion and garlic and sauté over high heat, stirring constantly. As soon as the eggplant mixture has cooked a bit, add the zucchini, tomato sauce, salt and pepper. Lower the heat and simmer about 15 minutes, then add the mushrooms and simmer for another 20 minutes. Remove from the heat and cool.

Follow the folding instructions on page 31.

Bake on a greased baking sheet in a preheated 375° F. oven until golden brown, about 20 minutes. Cool about 10 minutes before serving.

Makes about 30 triangles.

RED PEPPERS WITH OLIVES
MEDITERRANEAN

Combining the Mediterranean flavors of roasted sweet red peppers, garlic and olive oil, this makes a lovely light summer supper. If your guests like anchovies, this is one recipe that shows them off well. Or, serve anchovies on the side and each guest can top the pastry with as many as desired.

SHAPE   Short or Long Roll (page 32 or 36)

FILO   About ¼ pound

FOR BRUSHING FILO   Butter, melted
   Note: If you include anchovies in the filling, use unsalted butter.

FILLING
   4 sweet red peppers
   1½–2 tablespoons olive oil
   4 cloves garlic, minced
   1–2 tablespoons finely chopped fresh parsley
   ½ cup black olives, pitted and chopped
   4 hard-boiled eggs, each cut lengthwise into 6 wedges
   1 2-ounce can anchovy filets (optional)
   Freshly grated Asiago *or* Parmesan cheese

TO ASSEMBLE
Roast the red peppers (holding them with metal tongs) by placing them directly over the gas flame on top of the stove, turning them until the skin turns black all over. This should only take about 1 to 2 minutes. Put them in a paper bag to let them sweat for 5 or 10 minutes, then peel the skins under cold running water. Remove the seeds and white membranes and cut the peppers into thin strips. Heat the olive oil in a medium-sized skillet, add the red peppers and garlic and sauté for about 6 minutes, stirring frequently. When the peppers are tender, place them in a bowl and mix with the parsley and olives.

Follow the folding instructions for the shape you have chosen on page 32 or 36. If you're making the long rolls, use 3 sheets of filo instead of 2, placing one on top of the other and brushing each with melted butter.

To assemble the ingredients, first lay a strip of the red pepper mixture along the edge of the filo. Place the egg wedges on top of the peppers in a single row. If you're using the anchovies, lay them on top of the eggs. Sprinkle a little of the grated cheese on top of the filling. Continue with the folding instructions.

Bake in a preheated 375° F. oven until golden brown, about 30 minutes. Let rolls cool 15 minutes before serving.

Makes 2 long rolls or 6 short rolls.

Note: You can find the roasted and peeled sweet red peppers (called *peperonata*) in tins or glass jars at some supermarkets or delicatessens, but they are best when prepared fresh.

CABBAGE WITH CHORIZO

Old Eastern European strudels often had a savory stuffing such as crayfish, kidney, bacon, spinach or cabbage. To make a vegetarian entrée, omit the sausage in this *krautstrudel*.

SHAPE   Large Spiral or Ring Mold
   (page 39 or 48)

FILO   About ½ pound

FOR BRUSHING FILO   Butter, melted

FILLING

   3 Spanish *chorizo* sausages

   5 tablespoons olive oil

   2 onions, chopped

   5 cloves garlic, minced

   1 small head of cabbage, about 2
      pounds

   1 teaspoon dried dill *or* 2 teaspoons
      fresh dill

   ½ teaspoon paprika

   ½ teaspoon salt

   Freshly grated black pepper to taste

   1 cup sour cream

   2 tablespoons freshly grated Romano
      or Parmesan cheese

TO ASSEMBLE

Slice the *chorizo* into ½-inch pieces and fry on both sides until brown. Remove, drain on a towel and set aside. Heat the olive oil in a large skillet, add the onions and garlic and sauté until golden.

   Cut the cabbage into quarters and remove all of the core. Slice the cabbage finely and add to the sautéed onions. Over a high flame cook the cabbage, stirring constantly, until it is tender. (You may need to add more olive oil.) Transfer the cabbage mixture to a colander and let all of the excess liquid drain thoroughly. Then place in a large bowl and add the cooked *chorizo*, dill, paprika, salt and pepper. After the mixture has cooled a bit, mix in the sour cream and cheese.

   Follow the folding instructions for the shape you have chosen on page 39 or 48.

   Bake in a preheated 375° F. oven until golden brown, about 45 minutes. Let the pie cool 15 minutes before serving.

Serves 4 to 6 as an entrée.

BAKED CHILES RELLENOS
MEXICAN

I've always enjoyed Mexican food and especially *chiles rellenos,* but the traditional method of making them is time-consuming. I find that the taste and texture of filo works well with chiles and cheese. So, whenever I get hungry for that taste, I make this, my own version of *chiles rellenos.*

SHAPE Square or Rectangular Pan or Simple Round (page 46 or 50)

FILO About ½ pound for square pan; ¼ pound for simple round

FOR BRUSHING FILO Butter, melted

FILLING
2 4-ounce cans whole mild green chiles
5 eggs, beaten
¼ teaspoon salt
½ teaspoon ground cumin
1 cup grated Jack cheese

TO ASSEMBLE
Rinse the chiles under cold water and dry. Mix together the beaten eggs with the salt and cumin.

Follow the layering instructions for the shape you have chosen on page 46 or 50. After layering the bottom of the pan with filo, place the chiles over the filo. Then sprinkle the grated cheese evenly over the chiles and pour the egg mixture over all. Continue with the layering instructions.

Bake in a preheated 375° F. oven until the eggs are set and the top is golden brown, about 35 minutes. Let cool about 15 minutes before serving.

Serves 4 as an entrée.

BROCCOLI-TOFU ROLLS

SHAPE   Short or Long Roll (page 32 or 36)

FILO   About ¼ pound

FOR BRUSHING FILO
> Butter, melted
> Sesame seed (optional)

FILLING
> 5 dried Japanese (or Chinese) mushrooms
>
> ½ pound fresh broccoli
>
> 2 tablespoons peanut oil
>
> 1 onion, chopped
>
> 1 clove garlic, minced
>
> 6 water chestnuts, minced
>
> 7 ounces firm-style tofu, drained and cubed
>
> 2 tablespoons soy sauce
>
> ½ teaspoon or more chili oil
>
> 1 egg, beaten

TO ASSEMBLE

Soak the mushrooms in hot or boiling water for about 30 minutes. When softened, squeeze out the excess water. Slice them thinly, discarding the tough stems, and set aside. Remove the leaves and the tough bottom portion of the broccoli stalks. Cut the broccoli — florets and remaining stem — into small pieces and steam briefly, leaving the broccoli *al dente* and still very green. Set aside.

In a large skillet, heat the peanut oil, add the onion and sauté until golden. Add the garlic, mushrooms, water chestnuts, tofu, soy sauce and chili oil and sauté 5 minutes more. Then mix in the broccoli and remove from the heat. When the mixture has cooled slightly, stir in the beaten egg.

Follow the folding instructions for the shape you have chosen on page 32 or 36. If you wish, sprinkle a little sesame seed on top of the rolls.

Bake on a greased baking sheet in a preheated 375° F. oven until golden brown, about 25 minutes.

Makes 2 long rolls or 6 short rolls.

CORN FRITTERS
INDONESIAN

My Indonesian friend, Artie Moestopo, first introduced me to corn fritters, and since I've always had a great liking for corn, I immediately took the idea and turned it to my own purposes.

SHAPE   Triangle or Short Roll
     (page 31 or 32)

FILO   About ¾ pound

FOR BRUSHING FILO
     Butter, melted
     1 egg, beaten

FOR DEEP-FRYING   Light vegetable oil

FILLING
     2 cups fresh *or* frozen corn kernels,
        defrosted
     3–4 green onions, chopped
     1 clove garlic, minced
     1 tablespoon chopped celery leaf
     ¼ cup cooked chicken *or* shrimp *or*
        meat, chopped (optional)
     2 eggs, beaten
     Salt to taste

¼ teaspoon or more cayenne pepper
½ teaspoon ground cumin
¼ teaspoon ground coriander
½ cup freshly grated Parmesan cheese

TO ASSEMBLE
If using frozen corn, let the corn defrost in the refrigerator. Mix corn together with the rest of the ingredients.

Follow the folding instructions for the shape you have chosen on page 31 or 32. Using your finger, seal each fritter with a little beaten egg.

Gently place the fritters in hot (400° F.) oil a few at a time and deep-fry on both sides until golden brown. Remove and drain excess oil on a towel.

Makes about 16 fritters.

SAVORY PUMPKIN BAKE
MEDITERRANEAN

Inspired by *kolokithopita,* a pumpkin or squash pie traditional to the Peloponnesus, this is good as either a main course or a side dish for poultry and meats. In some parts of Greece it is also made without cheese, sweetened with honey and flavored with fresh mint, rather than summer savory and oregano.

SHAPE   Square or Rectangular Pan (page 46)

FILO   About ½ pound

FOR BRUSHING FILO

Butter, melted

1 egg yolk, beaten (for glazing top)

FILLING

2 cups fresh pumpkin puree (1 small, 5-pound pumpkin yields about 2½ cups)

3 tablespoons olive oil

2 onions, chopped

5 cloves garlic, minced

1 cup cooked bulgur (sometimes called *pilgouri, burghul* or *bulghur*)

1 teaspoon *Harissa* sauce (page 23)

1 teaspoon dried summer savory

1 teaspoon dried oregano

Salt and pepper to taste

3 eggs, beaten

1¼ cups freshly grated Parmesan or Romano cheese

TO ASSEMBLE

Bake a whole pumpkin in a 400° F. oven for about 45 minutes, until it is tender when pierced with a fork. Remove from the oven and cut in half. Scoop out the seeds and fibers and remove the skin. Puree pumpkin flesh in a blender or food mill. Place in a large bowl and set aside.

Heat the olive oil in a large skillet. Sauté the onion and garlic until golden. Add to the pumpkin puree and mix well. Then add the cooked bulgur, *Harissa* sauce, summer savory, oregano, salt, pepper, eggs and cheese.

Follow the folding instructions for the shape you have chosen on page 46. Brush the top of the pastry with the beaten egg yolk.

Bake in a preheated 375° F. oven until golden brown, about 30 minutes. Let cool 15 minutes before cutting.

Serves 6 as a side dish or vegetarian entrée.

For variation: In place of the pumpkin, you may substitute any of the yellow winter squashes, such as acorn, banana, butternut or Hubbard squash.

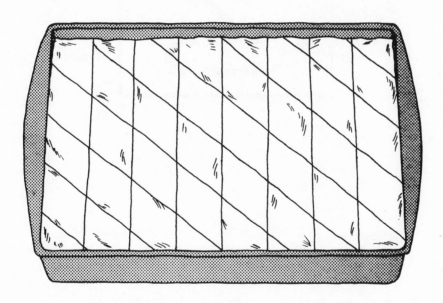

Fish

SHRIMP BOATS

These make an elegant brunch dish when made in the boat shape. For appetizers, make small triangles.

SHAPE   Boat or Triangle (page 34 or 31)

FILO   About ¾ pound

FOR BRUSHING FILO

Unsalted butter, melted

FILLING

1 tablespoon butter

½ pound fresh mushrooms, thinly sliced

3 green onions, chopped

8 ounces cream cheese, room temperature

Pepper to taste

1 clove garlic, finely minced

2 tablespoons finely chopped fresh parsley

1 teaspoon freshly squeezed lemon juice

½ teaspoon soy sauce

½ pound cooked shrimp (*or* substitute crab *or* tuna *or* salmon)

GARNISH FOR THE BOAT SHAPE

12 large mushrooms

Butter

Freshly grated Parmesan cheese

Parsley sprigs

TO ASSEMBLE

Melt the butter in a frying pan, add the mushrooms and green onions and cook for 2 to 3 minutes over medium heat, stirring constantly. Transfer the mushroom mixture to a colander, let it drain thoroughly and set aside.

In a bowl, mix together the cream cheese, pepper, garlic, parsley, lemon juice, soy sauce and shrimp. Add the drained mushroom mixture and mix well.

Follow the instructions for the shape you have chosen on page 34 or 31.

To garnish the boat shape, place 2 whole mushrooms in the center of each boat, brush the tops with a little melted butter and sprinkle some Parmesan cheese on top.

Bake on a greased baking sheet in a preheated 350° F. oven until golden brown, about 25 minutes. For the boat shape, decorate the mushroom garnish with a sprig of parsley when the boats come out of the oven. Serve immediately.

Makes 6 boats or 24 triangles.

SCALLOPS IN WINE AND CREAM SAUCE
FRENCH

Inspired by Coquilles St. Jacques, this recipe is especially good made in small appetizer shapes. The buttery filo is wonderful with the rich sweetness of the scallops and their cheese- and wine-flavored sauce.

SHAPE   Butterfly, Small Spiral or Double Spiral (page 37)

FILO   About ¾ pound

FOR BRUSHING FILO   Butter, melted

FILLING

1 pound scallops

½ cup extra-dry vermouth

Salt and white pepper to taste

8 tablespoons butter

1 pound fresh mushrooms, sliced

3–4 green onions, chopped

4 tablespoons flour

⅓ cup or more heavy cream

½ cup grated Swiss *or* Gruyère cheese

2 tablespoons fine bread crumbs

TO ASSEMBLE

In a heavy skillet, combine the scallops, vermouth, salt and white pepper. Bring to a boil, lower heat and simmer gently until the scallops turn white, 4 to 5 minutes. Drain the scallops, reserving the cooking liquid. Cut the scallops into small pieces.

Over medium heat, sauté the mushrooms and green onions in 4 tablespoons of the butter. Drain any excess liquid and set aside.

In a heavy skillet, melt 4 tablespoons of butter. Add the flour while stirring constantly with a wire whisk. Slowly mix in the reserved scallop/wine liquid and the heavy cream, continuing to whisk until you have a smooth, thick *roux*. If necessary, add a little more heavy cream. Remove from the heat and add the mushrooms, scallops, cheese and bread crumbs, mixing well.

Follow the folding instructions for the shape you have chosen on page 37.

Bake on a greased baking sheet in a preheated 350° F. oven until golden brown, about 25 minutes.

Serves 6 as an entrée.

EGGS WITH SHRIMP
FRENCH

A perfect French-inspired brunch dish.

SHAPE   Figure Eight (page 37)

FILO   About ½ pound

FOR BRUSHING FILO   Butter, melted

FILLING

    2 tablespoons butter

    3 green onions, chopped

    6 hard-boiled eggs, finely chopped

    1½ tablespoons finely chopped fresh
      parsley

    ¼ teaspoon chopped tarragon (fresh, if
      possible)

    1 tablespoon Dijon mustard

    ½ cup heavy cream

    1 cup cooked shrimp

    Salt and pepper to taste

    3–4 tablespoons freshly grated
      Parmesan cheese

TO ASSEMBLE

In a frying pan, melt the butter and sauté the green onions slightly. Remove from heat and add the chopped eggs, parsley, tarragon, mustard, heavy cream, shrimp, salt, pepper and Parmesan cheese and mix well.

Follow the folding instructions on page 37.

Bake on a greased baking sheet in a preheated 350° F. oven until golden brown, about 30 minutes. Garnish with a little fresh parsley inside the holes of the figure eight.

Makes 4 figure eight shapes.

SALMON MOUSSE

SHAPE   Fish (see below for instructions)

FILO   About 1 pound

FOR BRUSHING FILO

Unsalted butter, melted

1 egg, beaten (for glazing top)

FILLING

2 teaspoons butter

3–4 shallots, finely minced

1 pound salmon filets

1 cup heavy cream

3 ounces cream cheese, room
temperature

¼ teaspoon salt

Pinch of fresh nutmeg

Pinch of cayenne pepper

TOPPING

1 pint sour cream

1 tablespoon freshly squeezed
lemon juice

¼ teaspoon dill weed

2 teaspoons capers, drained

TO ASSEMBLE

Heat the butter in a small frying pan. Add the shallots and sauté lightly, then remove from heat and set aside. Check to be sure that all the bones and skin from the salmon are removed. Then, place salmon in a blender or food processor and grind it up thoroughly, slowly adding the heavy cream. When it is well ground, add the cream cheese, salt, nutmeg and cayenne pepper and blend well again. Transfer the salmon mixture to a bowl and add the sautéed shallots.

Find a piece of paper as big as 1 whole sheet of filo and, with scissors, cut out a rounded free-form fish. With this as your pattern, cut 16 whole sheets of filo into the same shape.

Lightly grease a large, baking sheet. Lay out 8 of the cut-out sheets of filo on the baking sheet, one on top of the other, brushing each sheet with butter before laying down the next. Spread the salmon mousse evenly over the filo, leaving a 1-inch margin around the edges. Cover the mousse

Continued on next page

with the remaining 8 sheets of filo, brushing each with butter. Seal the edges well with butter and, with your finger, apply a little of the beaten egg around the entire edge of the fish. Fold the edges over ½ inch to seal the fish completely. Brush the entire top of the fish with the beaten egg.

Bake in a 375° F. oven until golden brown, about 30 minutes. Let the mousse cool about 10 minutes before serving.

While it is cooling, prepare the topping by mixing together the sour cream, lemon juice, dill weed and capers. Cut the mousse into serving pieces and serve with a dollop of the sour cream topping over each piece.

Serves 6 to 8 as an entrée.

SMOKED SALMON PUFFS
JEWISH

SHAPE Triangle (page 31)

FILO About ¼ pound

FOR BRUSHING FILO Butter, melted

FILLING

8 ounces cream cheese, room temperature

1 tablespoon butter, room temperature

2½ tablespoons chopped lox *or* smoked salmon

TO ASSEMBLE

In a bowl, mix together the cream cheese, butter and smoked salmon.

Follow the folding instructions on page 31.

Bake on a greased baking sheet in a preheated 350° F. oven until golden brown, about 25 minutes. Let cool 15 minutes before serving.

Makes about 10 triangles.

CRAB CANNELLONI
ITALIAN

Anything that can be stuffed into a pasta shell can also be used as filling for filo. I have found that any number of cannelloni fillings work very well.

SHAPE   Short or Long Roll (page 32 or 36)

FILO   About ½ pound

FOR BRUSHING FILO   Butter, melted

FILLING
- 1½ tablespoons butter
- 1 pound fresh spinach with stems removed *or* 1 package frozen chopped spinach, defrosted
- 1 clove garlic, minced
- 1½ cups ricotta cheese
- 2 eggs
- 3 green onions, chopped
- ½ teaspoon salt
- ⅓ cup freshly grated Parmesan *or* Romano cheese
- ½ pound crab meat

TOPPING   Sour cream

TO ASSEMBLE

Melt the butter in a skillet and sauté the spinach and garlic for a few minutes until the spinach is slightly cooked, but still quite green. Drain in a colander and set aside.

In a bowl, mix together the rest of the ingredients. Then add the drained spinach.

Follow the folding instructions for the shape you have chosen on page 32 or 36.

Bake on a greased baking sheet in a preheated 350° F. oven until golden brown, about 30 minutes. Let the cannelloni cool 5 to 10 minutes before serving. Serve topped with a dollop of sour cream.

Makes 12 short rolls or 3 long rolls.

OYSTER RICE BALLS

Inspired by the Japanese *musubi,* rice balls are easy, inexpensive party hors d'oeuvres.

SHAPE　　Ball (page 43)

FILO　　About ⅓ pound

FOR BRUSHING FILO　　Butter, melted

FILLING

    1½ cups cooked Japanese rice (*or* leftover rice)
    1 can smoked oysters
    Swiss *or* Gruyère cheese

TO ASSEMBLE

Follow the folding instructions on page 43 . After you have buttered the top sheet of your filo, place about 1 tablespoon of the cooked rice in the center of the square. Place an oyster on top of the rice. Cut the cheese into thin, bite-size pieces and place 1 piece on top of the oyster. Continue with the folding instructions.

    Bake in a preheated 375° F. oven until golden brown, about 20 minutes. The balls may also be deep-fried.

Makes 14 balls.

FISH FILETS WITH GINGER AND LIME

SHAPE   Long Roll (page 36)

FILO   About ½ pound

FOR BRUSHING FILO   Butter, melted

FILLING

    2 shallots, minced

    1 teaspoon grated fresh ginger root

    1 teaspoon chopped zest of lime

    1 teaspoon freshly squeezed lime juice

    4 filets of snapper (*or* sole *or* bass
        or other fish of your choice)

GARNISH   1 lime, cut in wedges

TO ASSEMBLE

Mix together the shallots, ginger root, zest of lime and lime juice. Cut 4 whole sheets of filo in half horizontally. Stack the half-sheets and cover with clear plastic wrap or a damp cloth. Pick up 2 half-sheets and lay them out, one on top of the other. Brush top sheet with a little butter. Spread ¼ of the shallot mixture at the bottom edge of the filo. Place 1 fish filet on top of shallot mixture.

Now continue with the folding instructions on page 36 beginning with step 2. Repeat the process with the remaining fish filets and shallot mixture.

Bake on a greased baking sheet in a preheated 400° F. oven until golden brown, about 15 minutes. Serve immediately with lime wedges, or, if you wish, a melted butter and lime sauce.

Serves 4 as an entrée.

Chicken

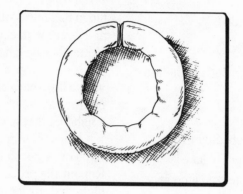

CHICKEN AND BROCCOLI ROLL

I recommend serving this as a main course for either lunch or dinner — it's quite elegant yet easy to prepare.

SHAPE   Rolled Spiral (page 40)

FILO   About ½ pound

FOR BRUSHING FILO   Butter, melted

FILLING

> 1 whole chicken *or* 2 whole chicken breasts
>
> 1 bunch broccoli
>
> Bread crumbs
>
> Freshly grated Parmesan cheese
>
> 1 pint sour cream
>
> Salt and pepper to taste

TO ASSEMBLE

Place chicken in a large pot. Add 1½ quarts water, cover and bring to a boil. Simmer for 1 hour until the chicken is tender. Remove it from the pot and let it cool a bit. Then skin and bone the chicken, and shred the meat into small strips. Set aside.

Cut off the tough stems of the broccoli. Divide the head of the broccoli into small florets and place in a saucepan. Steam briefly, leaving them *al dente* and still very green. Drain and set aside.

Spread half of the broccoli over the filo and sprinkle with a generous amount of Parmesan cheese. Mix the chicken together with the sour cream, salt and pepper to taste, and spread half of this mixture evenly over everything. Refer to page 40 for rolling instructions.

To make a second roll, repeat the process above using 4 more sheets of filo and the remaining ingredients.

Place the rolls on a greased baking sheet and bake in a preheated 375° F. oven until golden brown, 20 to 25 minutes. Let cool 15 minutes before cutting. To serve, cut into slices.

Serves 6 to 8 as an entrée.

LUMPIA WITH SPICY PEANUT SAUCE
INDONESIAN

Lumpia takes its name from the thin crepe-like pastry used to enclose a filling of vegetables often mixed with pork or shrimp. This simple but delicious Indonesian snack adapts well to filo. The pastries are good plain, but I like them even better served with the spicy peanut sauce.

Try making them with your favorite Chinese spring roll stuffing. The sauce is also good used on its own as a dip for raw vegetables.

SHAPE   Short Roll (page 32)

FILO   About 1 pound

FOR BRUSHING FILO
    Butter, melted
    1 egg, beaten

FILLING
    2 cups cooked chicken *or* turkey meat
        (*or* cooked pork *or* ham *or* shrimp)
    2 tablespoons peanut oil
    4 cloves garlic, minced
    1 large onion, chopped
    1 6½-ounce can bamboo shoots, thinly
        sliced
    1 teaspoon salt
    ½ teaspoon coarsely ground black
        pepper
    2 cups fresh bean sprouts

FOR DEEP-FRYING   Light vegetable oil

PEANUT SAUCE
    1½ tablespoons peanut oil
    4 cloves garlic, minced
    1 onion, chopped
    1 cup crunchy peanut butter
    1 tablespoon brown sugar
    1–1½ cups hot water or coconut juice
    3 tablespoons soy sauce
    1 tablespoon freshly squeezed lemon
        juice
    1–2 small dried hot chili peppers,
        minced
    Pepper to taste

TO ASSEMBLE

Chop the chicken or turkey meat into small pieces and set aside. Sauté the garlic and onion in peanut oil. Drain the liquid from the bamboo shoots and add them to the onion mixture along with the salt and pepper. Cook for about 3 minutes, stirring occasionally, then add the chopped meat and cook for about 1 minute longer. Remove from the heat and add the bean sprouts, mixing well.

Follow the folding instructions on page 32. Because the *lumpia* are deep-fried, seal the edges with a little beaten egg, using your fingers. After all the *lumpia* have been stuffed and folded, place them in the refrigerator while you prepare the peanut sauce.

TO MAKE THE PEANUT SAUCE

For the peanut sauce, heat the peanut oil in a frying pan. Sauté the garlic and onion until golden. Remove from the heat, then add the peanut butter and brown sugar. Slowly add the hot water or coconut juice, stirring until the sauce has a smooth consistency. Mix in the soy sauce, lemon juice, chiles and pepper. Set aside. Serve the sauce at room temperature.

Heat the vegetable oil to 375° F. for deep-frying. Fry the *lumpia* a few at a time, turning once, until golden brown. Drain on a towel to remove excess oil and serve immediately with peanut sauce on top.

Serves 6 to 8 as an appetizer.

Note: As a variation, try serving these with hot mustard instead of the peanut sauce, or have both available.

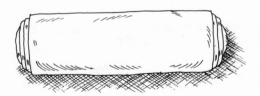

BESTILA
MOROCCAN

Bestila (sometimes, but incorrectly, spelled *bastilla*) is the elaborate pigeon pie that is traditional in Morocco. Of Andalusian origin, it is usually made with a paper-thin pastry very similar to filo called *warqa*. Described by the Moroccans as "food for a wedding," *bestila* may well be the supreme filo dish — a splendid creation of crisp filo, tender chicken (or, in the original version, pigeon) cooked in spices and layered with eggs and almonds with a final dusting of powdered sugar and cinnamon. The completed dish is well worth your time and effort; allow 3 to 4 hours preparation time.

    Bestila is a very festive dish, and is only for those who will savor every morsel and make this the sensuous experience it deserves to be. It is best eaten in the Moroccan manner — with the hands — and served with a refreshing Moroccan Orange Salad (page 138).

SHAPE   Elaborate Round
    (page 52)

FILO   About 1 pound

FOR BRUSHING FILO
    ½ pound unsalted butter, melted
    1 egg yolk, beaten (for glazing top)

FILLING
    5–6 tablespoons butter
    1 3½–4 pound chicken with liver and giblets *or* 4 pounds pigeon *or* pheasant
    1 large onion, chopped

4 tablespoons chopped fresh parsley
¼ teaspoon ground saffron *or* threads
1 teaspoon ground ginger
½ teaspoon ground cinnamon
½ teaspoon ground allspice
1 teaspoon ground cumin
1 teaspoon or less cayenne pepper
1½ cups water
7–8 large eggs, beaten
¾ cup blanched almonds, chopped
1 tablespoon sugar
½ teaspoon cinnamon

DECORATIVE GARNISH

    Powdered sugar

    Cinnamon

    6 whole cloves

    6 whole almonds

    2 bunches parsley

    1 fresh rose (of a brilliant color)

TO ASSEMBLE

In a large pot, melt 4 tablespoons of the butter, add the onion and sauté until golden. Mix in the chopped parsley, saffron, ginger, cinnamon, allspice, cumin and cayenne pepper. Then add the water and mix well. Now add the bird, including liver and giblets. Cover the pot, bring to a boil and simmer over low heat until tender, about 1 to 1½ hours, depending on the size of the bird. When the bird is done, remove it from the pot, saving the stock, and let it cool a bit. Then skin and bone it and shred the meat into strips. Set aside.

Remove 1½ cups of the reserved stock from the pot and set aside. Bring the remaining stock to a boil and, over very high heat, reduce it to just 4 or 5 tablespoons of glaze. Put the glaze in a separate bowl and set aside. Now return the 1½ cups of stock to the pot and bring it to a boil. Add the beaten eggs to the hot stock all at once, stirring constantly until the mixture is creamy and nearly set. (It should resemble the consistency of scrambled eggs.) Remove from the heat and immediately transfer to another bowl.

In a small frying pan, melt 1 to 2 tablespoons of butter. Add the chopped almonds and sauté them until lightly browned. In a bowl, mix them with sugar and cinnamon. Set aside.

Brush a large round pizza pan with melted butter. Follow the layering instructions on page 52. When you're ready to add the filling, sprinkle the almond mixture evenly in the pan. Spread the egg mixture over the almond mixture. Then place the strips of meat on top, spreading the glaze over the meat. Now continue with the layering instructions.

When you've finished layering the filo, brush the top of the pie with a beaten egg yolk. Bake in a preheated 350° F. oven until the pastry has risen and has turned a deep golden brown, about 45 minutes to 1 hour.

After the *bestila* is baked, sift a generous amount of powdered sugar on top; then dust a little cinnamon over the sugar. Decorate as shown below, placing a whole clove at the base of each almond. Surround the pie with a thick forest of parsley sprigs. Now place your fresh rose in the center. Let

Continued on next page

the *bestila* cool at least 30 minutes before cutting. It remains quite hot for a long time, so don't worry about it cooling. Now, with a very sharp knife, cut it into pieces like a pie and serve with Moroccan Orange Salad.

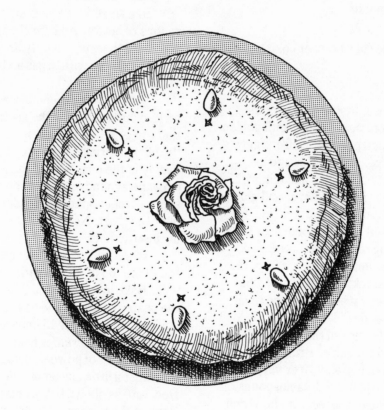

Meat

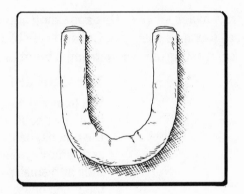

SANTA FE CHILI APPETIZERS

Best made into some of the smaller shapes, this appealing appetizer shows filo's affinity for even such hearty foods as chili. Try Cuban-style black beans, too, simmered with lots of garlic, fresh ground cumin and a bit of orange.

SHAPE   Triangle (page 31)

FILO   About 1 pound

FOR BRUSHING FILO   Butter, melted

FILLING

     1 pound lean ground beef

     2 onions, chopped

     1 bell pepper, chopped

     3 cloves garlic, minced

     1 16-ounce can whole tomatoes

     1 16-ounce can kidney beans

     1 tablespoon chili powder

     ½ teaspoon or less cayenne pepper

     1 teaspoon ground cumin

     2 teaspoons salt

     ½ teaspoon paprika

     1 bay leaf, broken in half

     ½ cup freshly grated Parmesan cheese

TO ASSEMBLE

In a heavy skillet, crumble the beef and brown without adding extra fat or oil. Add the onions, bell pepper and garlic to the pan and remove from heat. Then cut the tomatoes into small pieces and add them to the meat and onion mixture along with the tomato juice from the can. Rinse the kidney beans, drain thoroughly and add to the meat. Add the remainder of the ingredients, *except* the Parmesan cheese, and mix well. Cover the skillet, bring to a boil and simmer over a low flame for 1 hour. Remove from the heat. When the chili has cooled, add the Parmesan cheese.

Follow the folding instructions for the triangle on page 31. Bake in a preheated 375° F. oven until golden brown, about 20 minutes. Let cool a few minutes before serving.

Makes 35 appetizers.

SAVORY SAUSAGE AND TOMATO PIE

SHAPE   Square or Rectangular Pan, Simple Round (page 46 or 50)

FILO   About ¼ pound

FOR BRUSHING FILO

Unsalted butter, melted

1 egg, beaten (for glazing top)

FILLING

½ pound mild Italian sausage

2 large tomatoes

8 water chestnuts, chopped

1½ cups grated sharp cheddar cheese

½ cup mayonnaise

2 teaspoons Dijon mustard

Salt and pepper to taste

½ teaspoon dried sweet basil *or* 1 tablespoon chopped fresh basil

¼ cup finely chopped fresh parsley

TO ASSEMBLE

Remove the sausage from its casing. Crumble and sauté it in a small skillet until the sausage has cooked through. When done, pour boiling water over the sausage to cut grease, drain thoroughly and set aside. Peel the tomatoes, cut them in half and squeeze out all the seeds and liquid, leaving only the meat of the tomato. Chop them into small pieces and place in a strainer to drain any excess liquid. In a bowl, combine the water chestnuts, cheddar cheese, mayonnaise and mustard, mixing well.

Follow the folding instructions for the shape you have chosen on page 46 or 50. After you have layered the filo in the pan, spread the sausage evenly over it and cover with the drained tomatoes. Sprinkle salt, pepper, basil and parsley on top. Spread the cheese mixture over the top of everything. Now fold the filo over as instructed. Brush the top of the pie with a little of the beaten egg.

Bake in a preheated 375° F. oven until golden brown, about 45 minutes. Let the pie cool 20 minutes before cutting.

Serves 4 to 6 as an entrée.

CALZON
SPANISH

Calzon means "trouser," or in the plural, "bloomers," and this hearty peasant dish from Spain was originally a "trouser" of bread dough stuffed with sausages, vegetables, hard-boiled eggs and cheese. *Calzon* makes a wonderful picnic, brunch or lunch dish served with a green salad and rice pilaf. Be sure to let it cool a bit before serving so you can taste all the flavors.

It is also very successful when made with the many Italian *calzone* or pizza dough turnover fillings, such as prosciutto, cheese, olives, capers and anchovies.

SHAPE   Large Spiral or Ring Mold
(page 39 or 48)

FILO   About ½ pound

FOR BRUSHING FILO   Butter, melted

FILLING

1 pound mild Italian sausage

3 tablespoons olive oil

1 large onion, chopped

4 cloves garlic, minced

1 pound fresh spinach with stems removed *or* 1 package frozen chopped spinach, defrosted

3 hard-boiled eggs, chopped

1 cup freshly grated Parmesan cheese

½ teaspoon dried sweet basil *or* 1 tablespoon chopped fresh basil

½ teaspoon dried oregano *or* 1½ teaspoons chopped fresh oregano

Salt and pepper to taste

TO ASSEMBLE

Remove the sausage from the casings, crumble and cook thoroughly in a frying pan. When done, pour boiling water over the sausage to cut grease, drain thoroughly and set aside.

In a large frying pan, heat the olive oil, add the onion and sauté until golden. Add the garlic and the spinach, cooking rapidly until there is no water left in the pan. Now mix in the rest of the ingredients, remove the pan from the heat and set aside.

Follow the folding instructions for the shape you have chosen on page 39 or 48.

For the large spiral shape, bake in a preheated 350° F. oven until golden brown, about 45 minutes. For the ring mold, bake in a preheated 375° F. oven until golden brown, about 1 hour. Remove from the oven and let cool in the pan at least 10 minutes. Then turn it out onto a baking sheet and return it to the oven for another 5 minutes or until it becomes crispy.

Serves 6 as an entrée.

SPICY MEAT-FILLED ROLLS
LATIN AMERICAN

All over Latin America you'll find some form of *empanada,* or little turnover made with fillings based on the traditional local cuisine. When making these spicy rolls for a party, it's fun to make up several small bowls of filling, each with a slightly different palette of ingredients. Add chopped green olives to some, *chorizo,* orange peel, a little fresh coriander, strips of bright pimento and fresh chili to others.

SHAPE   Short Roll or Loop
    (page 32 or 38)

FILO   About ¾ pound

FOR BRUSHING FILO   Butter, melted

FILLING
    1–2 tablespoons olive oil
    1 small onion, chopped
    2 cloves garlic, minced
    ½ pound lean ground beef
    2–3 tablespoons raisins
    ¼ teaspoon salt
    ½ teaspoon paprika
    ¼ teaspoon ground cumin
    1–2 small dried hot red chiles, minced
    6 green olives, pitted and chopped
    2 hard-boiled eggs, each cut lengthwise
        into 8 wedges

TOPPING
    Sour cream
    Paprika

Continued on next page

TO ASSEMBLE
Heat the olive oil in a medium-sized skillet. Add the onion and sauté until golden. Mix in the garlic. Add the meat and crumble it, stirring constantly, until it is cooked through. Add the raisins, salt, paprika, cumin, chiles and olives. Mix well and remove from the heat.

Follow the folding instructions for the shape you have chosen on page 32 or 38. As you place the meat filling in each pastry, top it with 1 or 2 egg wedges.

Bake in a preheated 375° F. oven until golden brown, about 20 minutes. Serve hot with a dollop of sour cream and a sprinkling of paprika on top of each roll.

Makes 7 loops or 14 short rolls.

BOUREKAKIA
GREEK

In Greece, they are called *bourekia* or *bourekakia*. In Turkey, they are called *börek*. These little meat and vegetable turnovers with a spicy filling were introduced to Greece from Turkey at the time of the Ottoman empire. Mine are made with lamb, curry, eggplant, tomato and currants.

SHAPE   Triangle or Short Roll,
   Square or Rectangular Pan
   (page 31, 32 or 46)

FILO   1 pound for short roll or triangle;
   about ½ pound for square or
   rectangular pan

FOR BRUSHING FILO
   Butter, melted
   1 egg, beaten
   ⅛ teaspoon ground saffron

FILLING
   1 tablespoon olive oil
   1 tablespoon butter
   1 large onion, chopped
   5 cloves garlic, minced
   1 pound lean ground lamb
   1 8-ounce can tomato sauce
   ½ teaspoon salt
   ¼ teaspoon pepper
   ½ teaspoon cinnamon

   ½ teaspoon allspice
   4 teaspoons or more curry powder
   ¼ cup currants
   Water, as needed
   Olive oil, for sautéing eggplant
   1 large eggplant, cubed

TO ASSEMBLE

Heat olive oil and butter in a large skillet. Add the onion and sauté until golden. Mix in the garlic. Crumble the lamb and add it to the onion mixture, then cook until it is done. Add the tomato sauce, salt, pepper, cinnamon, allspice, curry and currants. Bring it to a boil, then simmer over low heat, uncovered, for 30 minutes. Stir occasionally, adding a little water to the pan if the meat mixture starts to stick to it.

   While the lamb mixture is cooking, heat some olive oil in a separate frying pan. When the oil is hot, add the cubed eggplant and sauté over high heat stirring frequently until the eggplant is browned on all sides and

Continued on next page

cooked through. Add the eggplant to the cooked lamb mixture.

In a small bowl, mix together the beaten egg and the saffron. Cover and set aside.

Follow the folding instructions for the shape you have chosen on page 31, 32 or 46.

Brush the top of the pastry with the egg/saffron mixture.

Bake in a preheated 400° F. oven until golden brown, about 30 minutes. Let the pastry cool about 10 minutes before serving.

Serves 4 to 6 as an entrée.

MOUSSAKA
GREEK

When my aunt Niki first showed me how to make *moussaka* in Greece it was a day-long process. She is a careful and exacting cook, and I watched her painstakingly squeeze each eggplant slice by hand to remove the bitter juices. As superb as this *moussaka* was, I felt that spending 8 hours in the kitchen to make one dish was a bit too much.

Later, when I made it myself and implemented a few shortcuts to my aunt's method, I found it just as delicious. Instead of squeezing each eggplant slice you can sprinkle salt on them and place them on a towel or in a colander for about 1 hour to let the bitter juices drain. Then rinse them with cold water and pat each slice dry with a towel.

Moussaka continues to be a dish I enjoy making for friends and family, and it makes a marvelous main course wrapped in filo, with or without the customary custard topping.

SHAPE   Square or Rectangular Pan
(page 46)

FILO   About ½ pound

FOR BRUSHING FILO   Olive oil

FILLING

2 medium-sized eggplants

Olive oil

2 onions, chopped

3 garlic cloves, minced

1 pound lean ground lamb *or* beef

8 ounces tomato puree

Salt and pepper to taste

1 tablespoon cinnamon

¼ cup dry red wine

About ½ cup freshly grated Parmesan
or *kefalotiri* cheese

TO ASSEMBLE

Peel and cut the eggplants into ½-inch-thick slices. As explained above, salt and drain the bitter juices from the eggplant slices, then rinse and pat dry. Brush each slice lightly on each side with a little olive oil. Place on a baking sheet and bake in a preheated 400° F. oven until tender, then remove and set aside.

In a heavy skillet, heat some olive oil and sauté the onions and garlic over medium heat until golden. Add the ground meat and cook, crumbling it with a spoon. Then add the tomato puree, salt, pepper, cinnamon and wine. Simmer about 45 minutes over low heat. When done, sprinkle a little grated cheese into the meat mixture to soak up any excess liquid. Set aside.

Brush an 8½-inch by 12½-inch baking pan with olive oil. It is critical that the pan be at least 2 inches deep. Follow the folding instructions on page 46. To add the filling, first lay in half of the eggplant slices, then all of the meat mixture, followed by the remainder of the eggplant. Sprinkle Parmesan cheese over the top. If you've made the custard topping, use this as the final layer of the filling. Then continue with the filo layers according to the instructions.

Bake in a preheated 350° F. oven until golden brown, about 1 hour.

Serves 6 to 8 as an entrée.

CUSTARD TOPPING (Optional)

⅓ cup butter

½ cup flour

2 cups milk

Pinch of salt

⅛ teaspoon freshly grated nutmeg

½ cup freshly grated Parmesan *or
kefalotiri* cheese

6 eggs, beaten

Continued on next page

TO MAKE THE CUSTARD TOPPING

Melt the butter in a saucepan and mix in the flour with a wire whisk, beating constantly. Slowly blend in the milk, continuing to whisk, until the custard thickens. Remove it from the heat and mix in the salt, nutmeg and grated cheese. Then slowly add the custard to the beaten eggs, whisking continuously to prevent the eggs from curdling. Set aside.

LIVER PATE APPETIZERS
FRENCH

SHAPE   Triangle (page 31)

FILO   About ⅓ pound

FOR BRUSHING FILO   Butter, melted

FILLING

    3 tablespoons butter

    ½ pound chicken livers

    2–3 tablespoons marsala (*or* sherry *or* madeira)

    ¼ teaspoon salt

    ¼ teaspoon ground cloves

    ¼ teaspoon ground mace *or* nutmeg

    ¼ teaspoon or less cayenne pepper

    ½ small onion, finely chopped

TO ASSEMBLE

In a frying pan, melt 2 tablespoons of the butter. Sauté the chicken livers until they begin to firm but are still pink inside. Puree them in a blender along with the rest of the ingredients, *except* the onion. Transfer to a bowl and set aside. Sauté the onions in 1 tablespoon butter until golden, then add to the liver mixture.

Follow folding instructions on page 31.

Bake in a preheated 375° F. oven until golden brown, 20 to 25 minutes. Let cool 15 minutes before serving.

Makes 12 triangles.

BRIK BIL LAHM
TUNISIAN

Brik (pronounced *breek*) are a favorite street food in Tunisia and much of North Africa where they are made with *malsuqua* or *warqa,* a thin dough similar in texture to filo, formed into small round sheets. *Brik* is the Tunisian pronunciation of *börek* (page 105).

These deep-fried turnovers are filled with ground lamb or sometimes tuna and a whole raw egg. Tunisians also make a sweet type of *brik* stuffed with sweetened ground almonds flavored with orange peel. The fried turnovers, triangular in shape, are served with a sugar syrup, often garnished with walnuts, hazelnuts or sesame seed.

Briwat (sometimes spelled *braewat*) are North African pastries made with the same type of dough and filled with a variety of stuffings such as chicken, eggs or sometimes anchovies. Sweet *briwat* are stuffed with almond paste and dipped in honey.

SHAPE   This is the only recipe that calls for this particular round shape. Read the instructions below for wrapping the *brik*. If you like, you may substitute the triangle shape instead. You must, however, make each triangle 3 times larger than the regular-sized triangle.

FILO   About ¾ pound

FOR BRUSHING FILO
Unsalted butter, melted
1 egg, beaten

FILLING
1 pound lean lamb, ground or shredded
4 green onions, finely chopped
½ cup finely chopped fresh parsley
½ teaspoon salt

1 tablespoon butter
¼ teaspoon ground cumin
¾–1 teaspoon *Harissa* sauce (page 23), *or* you may substitute ¼ teaspoon cayenne pepper *or* Tabasco sauce
1 tablespoon fine bread crumbs *or* freshly grated Parmesan cheese (optional)
8 small eggs

Continued on next page

FOR DEEP-FRYING

Light vegetable oil, mixed with about ¼ cup olive oil for flavor

FOR SERVING   8 lemon wedges

TO ASSEMBLE

Mix together the lamb, onions, parsley and salt. In a medium-sized skillet melt the butter. Crumble the lamb mixture and sauté it, stirring until the lamb has cooked through. Remove from the heat and transfer it to a bowl. Add the cumin, *Harissa* sauce and the optional bread crumbs or cheese.

Cut the whole sheets of filo in half, horizontally. Stack all of the filo sheets together and cover with clear plastic wrap or a slightly damp cloth. To assemble each turnover, take 3 sheets of filo together and cut out a circle. Very lightly brush each circle with melted butter and stack one on top of the other. Spoon 4 to 5 tablespoons of the lamb mixture onto one half of the filo circle. Make a hollow or well in the lamb mixture and break 1 egg into it, being careful not to break the yolk. Fold the remaining half of the filo over

the lamb and egg. Use your finger to spread a little of the beaten egg on all the edges of the filo to seal it. Fold the edges over slightly to ensure that the *brik* will not open while being deep-fried. Repeat until you have used up all of the lamb mixture.

Heat the oil in a heavy, deep skillet or wok. When the oil is very hot, but not smoking, gently slide in 1 turnover at a time. (If you can manage to do 2 comfortably, you may.) Gently push the turnover down into the oil, spooning oil over it constantly. When the bottom side is golden brown, turn it over to cook on the other side. This should take only 2 to 3 minutes for each turnover. Be careful not to overcook the egg — the yolk should be runny. With a slotted spoon or spatula, remove the *brik* from the oil and drain thoroughly on a towel.

Serve the *brik* while they are still hot. Just before serving, poke a few holes in the top with a fork. Serve with a lemon wedge. Each guest should squeeze lemon juice over the top of the *brik*.

Serves 6 to 8 as an entrée (about 8 brik).

CHINESE DUMPLINGS

These may be baked or deep-fried; they're excellent either way.

SHAPE   Short Roll (page 32)

FILO   About ¾ pound

FOR BRUSHING FILO

Unsalted butter, melted

FILLING

3–4 dried Chinese mushrooms

½ head Chinese cabbage, finely chopped

1 teaspoon salt

½ pound ground pork

6–8 water chestnuts, chopped

3 green onions, chopped

1 clove garlic, minced

½ teaspoon grated fresh ginger root

1½ tablespoons soy sauce

1½ teaspoons Chinese-style sesame oil

1 egg, beaten

SAUCE FOR DIPPING DUMPLINGS

¼ cup soy sauce

1 tablespoon white vinegar

½ teaspoon sugar

½ teaspoon Chinese-style sesame oil

Dash of chili oil to taste

Grated fresh ginger root to taste

1 teaspoon chopped fresh coriander (Chinese parsley) (optional)

TO ASSEMBLE

Pour boiling water over the mushrooms to cover, and soak for about 30 minutes. Drain and squeeze out excess water, slice them into thin strips, discard the stems and set aside. Place the cabbage in a large bowl and mix in the salt. Set aside for 30 minutes stirring occasionally. Then remove all the excess water from the cabbage by squeezing it with your hands. Drain and set aside.

In an ungreased skillet, crumble the pork and cook it along with the mushrooms, water chestnuts, green onions, garlic and ginger. When the pork is cooked through, transfer the mixture to a bowl. Add the soy sauce, sesame oil, egg and drained cabbage and mix well.

Follow the folding instructions on page 32.

Bake on a greased baking sheet in a

Continued on next page

preheated 375° F. oven until golden brown, about 25 minutes. (If you deep-fry the dumplings, be sure to seal the edge of the filo with a little beaten egg, using your fingers. Deep-fry in hot 400° F. oil until golden brown on both sides. Drain the excess oil on a towel.)

TO MAKE DIPPING SAUCE
Mix together all the ingredients in a small bowl.

Makes about 14 dumplings.

SWEET AND SOUR PORK BALLS
CHINESE

SHAPE   Ball (page 43)

FILO   About ½ pound

FOR BRUSHING FILO
Butter, melted
1 egg, beaten

FILLING
1 pound ground pork
5 green onions, chopped
6 water chestnuts, finely chopped
1 egg
2 teaspoons soy sauce
2 tablespoons peanut oil
½ cup sugar
⅓ cup white vinegar

6 tablespoons water
1 tablespoon soy sauce
¼ cup or more chicken broth
Grated fresh ginger root to taste
1–2 tablespoons cornstarch mixed with a little cold water

FOR DEEP-FRYING   Light vegetable oil

TO ASSEMBLE

Mix together the pork, green onions, water chestnuts, egg and soy sauce and shape into little balls. In a heavy frying pan, heat the peanut oil, add the pork balls and fry on all sides until browned. Remove them from the heat and drain on a towel.

In a saucepan, combine the sugar, vinegar, water, soy sauce, chicken broth, ginger root and cornstarch. Bring to a boil, stirring constantly. As soon as the sauce thickens, add the browned pork balls, lower heat and simmer about 40 minutes. Let the pork balls cool before wrapping them in filo with some of their sauce.

Follow folding instructions on page 43, sealing each ball with a little beaten egg. Gently place the balls, a few at a time, in hot 375° F. oil and deep-fry until golden brown. Remove and drain excess oil on a towel.

Makes about 24 balls.

STUFFED BEEF ROLL
PHILIPPINE

Versions of this stuffed, rolled flank steak appear wherever the Spanish established their colonies — from Cuba and the Caribbean to Central America and South America all the way to the tip of Patagonia. This recipe comes from the Philippines and makes a spectacular appetizer or main course. Leftovers make great picnic fare.

SHAPE   Long Roll (page 36)

FILO   About ⅓ pound

FOR BRUSHING FILO

> Butter, melted
> 1 egg, beaten (for glazing top)

FILLING

> 1 flank steak (butterflied lengthwise), about 2½ pounds
>
> ½ cup white vinegar
>
> 2 tablespoons soy sauce
>
> 4 cloves garlic, finely minced
>
> 3 hot Italian sausages, with casings removed
>
> 1 egg
>
> ½ cup raisins *or* currants
>
> 1 5-ounce jar Spanish stuffed olives, drained and coarsely chopped
>
> 4–5 hard-boiled eggs
>
> 4 ounces cooked ham, cut into thin strips

TO ASSEMBLE

Trim all excess fat from the flank steak and place it in a bowl. Mix together the vinegar, soy sauce and garlic and pour over the meat. Cover and refrigerate. This should marinate at least 24 hours — 2 to 3 days are even better.

     After marinating, pat the flank steak dry with a towel. In a bowl, mix together the sausage meat, egg, raisins or currants and olives. Peel the hard-boiled eggs and place them in a single line, lengthwise, along the center of the flank steak. Cover the eggs with the sausage mixture. Lay the strips of ham on top of the entire filling. Roll up the flank carefully and tie it with string or sew together with a butcher's needle. Place roll seam side down in a large ungreased baking pan so all the juices can drain out. Cover with foil and bake in a 350° F. oven for 1 hour. Remove from oven and let it cool a bit. Then cover and refrigerate the roll overnight. This way it will keep its shape when the string is removed.

After taking the beef roll out of the refrigerator, remove all the string and any fat or juices clinging to the meat. Continue with the folding instructions on page 36, but instead of using only 2 sheets of filo, use 6 sheets, brushing each with butter.

Before placing the filo-covered roll in the oven, brush the top with a little of the beaten egg. Bake in a 375° F. oven until golden brown, about 25 minutes. Let it cool about 15 minutes before cutting.

Serves 6 as an entrée.

Desserts

BAKLAVA
IRANIAN

Though most Middle Eastern countries make a version of *baklava,* I think this is the best. Most *baklava* is too sweet for my taste, so I have cut down on the sugar by more than half and added more almonds. It is flavored with freshly ground cardamom and perfumed with a touch of rose water. This *baklava* is superb when it's eaten while still warm from the oven. If you're not serving it right away, reheat it in the oven for a few minutes before serving.

The Tunisians make a kind of *baklava* called *lourta* with round sheets of buttered *malsuqua* dough layered with mixed ground almonds, walnuts and hazelnuts. And in an Ethiopian restaurant, a friend was once served a *baklava* made with peanuts!

SHAPE   Square or Rectangular Pan
  (page 46)

FILO   About ¾ pound

FOR BRUSHING FILO
  ½ pound unsalted butter, melted

FILLING
  2 cups blanched almonds, chopped
  ½ cup or less sugar
  ½ teaspoon freshly ground cardamom

SYRUP TOPPING
  ¾ cup sugar
  ½ cup water
  2 tablespoons rose water

TO ASSEMBLE
Mix the almonds, sugar and cardamom together in a bowl.

Follow the layering instructions for the shape you have chosen on page 46.

Bake in a preheated 350° F. oven until golden brown, about 1 hour.

While the *baklava* is baking, prepare the syrup topping by mixing the sugar and water together in a saucepan. When it comes to a boil, immediately lower the heat and simmer for about 8 minutes. Remove from the heat and let it cool. Then, after it has cooled, add the rose water. Set aside.

When the *baklava* comes out of the oven, pour the cooled syrup evenly over the top and place back in the oven for 1 to 2 minutes. Let it cool at least 1 hour before serving.

Makes about 16 pieces.

BAKLAVA
GREEK

In Greece, *baklava* is usually made with walnuts or almonds, or a combination of both, and is prepared for special holidays and festive occasions. The honey syrup is flavored with cinnamon and cloves, rather than cardamom and rose water.

SHAPE   Square or Rectangular Pan
   (page 46)

FILO   About ¾ pound

FOR BRUSHING FILO
   ½ pound unsalted butter, melted

FILLING
   2 cups walnuts, chopped
   ¼ cup sugar (optional)
   1 tablespoon cinnamon

SYRUP TOPPING
   ½ cup sugar
   1 cup honey
   2 teaspoons freshly squeezed lemon
      juice
   ½ cup water
   1 cinnamon stick
   ½ teaspoon whole cloves
   1 teaspoon vanilla

TO ASSEMBLE
Mix together the walnuts, sugar and cinnamon in a bowl.

Follow the layering instructions for the shape you have chosen on page 46.

Bake in a preheated 350° F. oven until golden brown, about 1 hour.

While the *baklava* is baking, prepare the syrup topping by combining all of the above ingredients in a saucepan. Bring it to a boil, lower heat and simmer about 10 minutes. Remove from the heat, let cool and set aside.

When the *baklava* comes out of the oven, pour the cooled syrup evenly over the top and place it back in the oven for 1 to 2 minutes. Let it cool at least 1 hour before serving.

Makes about 16 pieces.

CHOCOLATE PISTACHIO NUT PASTRY

SHAPE   Triangle or Ball (page 31 or 43)

FILO   About ¼ pound

FOR BRUSHING FILO

Unsalted butter, melted

FILLING

¾ cup semi-sweet chocolate chips

½ cup raw pistachio nuts

TOPPING

Freshly whipped cream

TO ASSEMBLE

In a bowl mix together the chocolate chips and pistachio nuts for the filling.

Follow the folding instructions for the shape you have chosen on page 31 or 43.

Bake in a preheated 400° F. oven until golden brown, about 25 minutes. Let cool about 5 minutes before serving.

Serve with freshly whipped cream, barely sweetened, and flavored with a dash of brandy.

Serves 8.

KOPENHAYI
GREEK

This rich, elegant dessert was specially created in honor of King George I, a prince of Denmark who was elected to the throne of Greece in 1863. The Danish influence of almond paste merged with the Greek honey pastry to create the *Kopenhayi* or "Copenhagen."

As a child, I remember my dearest aunt, Maria Haniotis, making this at her Greek restaurant in Mount Clemens, Michigan. The restaurant was situated in an enchanting Victorian setting with grape-laden vines, picnic tables, and, usually, children playing. Inside, the elderly Greek men sipped their coffee or played cards or their mandolins while the women chatted and laughed with each other. I remember with nostalgia the wonderful aromas that emanated from her kitchen and filled the country neighborhood. To this day, I have never tasted *Kopenhayi* (or any other Greek pastry for that matter) better than my Aunt Maria's. This is her recipe, with minor changes — I cut down on the sugar and added a touch of cognac. It is best served warm from the oven with a cup of strong Greek coffee. (See the recipe for Greek-style coffee on page 137.)

SHAPE   Square or Rectangular Pan
  (page 46)

FILO   About ½ pound

FOR BRUSHING FILO
  ½ pound unsalted butter, melted

FILLING
  8-ounce can almond paste*
  ¼ cup sugar (optional)
  4 eggs
  2 tablespoons brandy *or* cognac
  ¼ teaspoon cinnamon

1 heaping teaspoon flour
½ rounded teaspoon baking powder

SYRUP TOPPING
  1 cup honey
  ½ cup water
  2 teaspoons freshly squeezed lemon
    juice
  Strips of orange peel from 1 orange
  1 cinnamon stick
  ½ teaspoon whole cloves

*If you would like to make your own, see instructions in the recipe for Mhannsha on page 134.

TO ASSEMBLE

With a fork, crumble the almond paste in a large bowl and mix in the sugar. Using an electric mixer, add the eggs one at a time, beating until thick and creamy. Then beat in the brandy, cinnamon, flour and baking powder.

Follow the layering instructions for the shape you have chosen on page 46 . But do not cut this pastry until *after* it comes out of the oven!

Bake in a preheated 350° F. oven until golden brown, about 50 minutes.

While the pastry is baking, prepare the syrup topping by mixing together all of the above ingredients in a saucepan. Bring it to a boil, then immediately lower the heat and simmer about 8 minutes. Remove from the heat, cool and set aside.

When the *Kopenhayi* comes out of the oven, pour the cooled syrup evenly over the top and place it back in the oven for 1 to 2 minutes. Let cool 1 hour before serving.

Makes about 16 pieces.

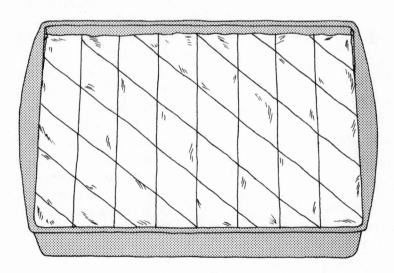

GALATOBOUREKO
GREEK

Galataboureko is a delicious pastry with a delicately sweetened custard filling. Although the use of a custard between layers of filo is characteristically Greek, there is also a Turkish folk recipe for a similar pastry called *kaymak baklavasi*.

Galatoboureko should be served at room temperature and eaten the same day it is baked. If, in the unlikely case that you do have some left, be sure to refrigerate it.

SHAPE   Square or Rectangular Pan
(page 46)

FILO   About ½ pound

FOR BRUSHING FILO
½ pound or less unsalted butter, melted

FILLING
1 quart milk
½ cup sugar
½ cup farina
2 tablespoons butter
6 eggs, lightly beaten
1 teaspoon vanilla

SYRUP TOPPING
1 cup honey
½ cup or less water
1 cinnamon stick
½ teaspoon whole cloves

A few strips of fresh orange peel
Juice from half a lemon *or* lime

TO ASSEMBLE
In a saucepan, combine the milk, sugar, farina, butter and beaten eggs. Cook over low heat, stirring constantly, until the mixture thickens, about 10 to 15 minutes. Remove from the heat and mix in the vanilla. Set aside.

Continue with the layering instructions on page 46. Do not cut this pastry until *after* it comes out of the oven!

Bake in a preheated 350° F. oven until golden brown and custard is set, about 50 minutes.

While the pastry is baking, prepare the honey syrup topping by mixing together all of the above ingredients in a saucepan. When the syrup comes to a boil, immediately lower the heat and simmer about 8 minutes. Remove from the heat, let the syrup cool and set aside.

When the pastry comes out of the oven, cut with a very sharp knife into diamond- or square-shaped pieces and pour the cooled syrup over the hot pastry. Let the *galatoboureko* cool at least 2 hours before serving.

Makes about 16 pieces.

KYTHONI
GREEK

In Greece, when guests drop in for a visit, *kythoni* (quince preserves) is traditionally served, along with a cup of Greek coffee and a glass of water. Fresh quince is available only in the fall; however, you can find prepared quince preserves in jars in Greek or Middle Eastern groceries any time of the year. If you buy it already prepared, it makes a fast, easy and unusual dessert, delicious when served with freshly whipped cream or yogurt. For variation, try using other fruit preserves.

SHAPE Triangle or Short Roll
  (page 31 or 32)

FILO About ¾ pound

FOR BRUSHING FILO
  Unsalted butter, melted

FILLING
  ½ pound fresh quince
  1 cup sugar
  ½ cup or less water

1 stick cinnamon
4 whole cloves
1 rose geranium leaf* (optional)
2 teaspoons freshly squeezed lemon
  juice

TO ASSEMBLE
Peel and core the quince, but do not discard the peel and cores. Wrap them in a cheese-cloth and tie with a piece of string. Grate the flesh of the quince into long, thin strips.

*These are not usually available commercially; just pick a leaf from the rose geranium in your garden.

Continued on next page

Place the quince, sugar, water, cinnamon stick, cloves and optional geranium leaf in a saucepan. Bring to a boil, lower heat and place the cheesecloth bag in the pan; the peels give the preserves a fine red color. Simmer on low heat, stirring frequently, until the quince is tender and the syrup has a thick consistency. (It should be thick enough to coat the back of a spoon.) Remove from the heat and add the lemon juice. Transfer to a bowl and remove the cheesecloth bag, cinnamon stick, cloves and optional leaf from the preserves. Let cool thoroughly.

Follow the folding instructions for the shape you have chosen on page 31 or 32

Bake in a preheated 375° F. oven until golden brown, about 20 minutes. Let the pastries cool for 15 minutes, then serve with freshly whipped cream or yogurt.

Serves 8.

APPLE STRUDEL
AUSTRIAN

The Czech word for strudel, *zavin,* means whirlpool. This conjures up an image of a "whirlpool" of filo rolled up with sliced apples, raisins, almonds and spices. In Northern Italy, pine nuts are used in apple strudel and, in parts of Eastern Europe, strudels are made with quince, cherries or plums as well.

SHAPE   Long Roll (page 36)

FILO   About ¾ pound

FOR BRUSHING FILO
Unsalted butter, melted

FILLING
¼ cup seedless raisins *or* currants
2 tablespoons dark rum

6 cups peeled, cored and thinly sliced tart apples
½ cup blanched almonds, chopped
¾ cup sugar
1 teaspoon cinnamon
½ teaspoon ground cloves
½ cup fine bread crumbs

TOPPING

Powdered sugar

Freshly whipped cream flavored with a
dash of rum

TO ASSEMBLE

Mix the raisins with the rum. Cover and let
them stand for at least 2 hours. In a large
bowl, mix together the apples, almonds,
sugar, cinnamon and ground cloves. Add the
rum-soaked raisins.

On a clean, flat surface, place 6 whole
sheets of filo, one on top of the other, brushing each with melted butter. Sprinkle ¼ cup
of the bread crumbs over the entire surface.
Place half of the apple mixture at the bottom
edge of the strip. Now follow the folding
instructions on page 36, beginning with
instruction number 2. Repeat this process
using the remainder of the ingredients to
make another roll. (If you prefer, you may
make individual strudel rolls by following the
short roll instructions on page 32, sprinkling
a fine, even layer of bread crumbs over the
surface of the buttered filo strips before
placing the apple mixture at the bottom of
the strip.)

Bake in a preheated 375° F. oven until
golden brown, about 45 minutes. Sprinkle
the top with powdered sugar. Let the
strudel cool 1 hour before serving. Serve
with whipped cream.

Makes 2 rolls.

CHOCOLATE SOUFFLE
FRENCH

You can adapt this idea to any of your favorite soufflés — try a Grand Marnier soufflé or a summery lemon, orange or peach soufflé.

SHAPE   Soufflé (page 44)

FILO   About ¼ pound

FOR BRUSHING FILO   Butter, melted

FILLING

    3 squares semi-sweet baking chocolate

    1 cup milk

    ½ cup sugar

    3 tablespoons butter

    3 tablespoons flour

    2 tablespoons brandy

    4 eggs, separated, room temperature

TO ASSEMBLE

Grate the chocolate and place it in a saucepan with the milk and sugar. Heat slowly, stirring, until the chocolate melts, and set aside. In another saucepan, melt the butter. With a wire whisk, mix in the flour. Stirring constantly, slowly add the hot milk mixture and cook over low heat until thickened. Remove from the heat and add the brandy.

In a bowl, beat the egg yolks lightly. Slowly add the slightly cooled milk mixture to the yolks and mix well. Beat the egg whites until stiff. (If you have extra whites, add them.) Mix ⅓ of the whites with the chocolate mixture, then gently fold in the rest.

Butter a 2-quart soufflé dish and follow the folding instructions on page 44.

Bake in a preheated 350° F. oven for about 45 minutes. Serve at once by cutting through the filo with a sharp knife, then spooning out portions. It's delicious accompanied with freshly whipped cream spiked with a little brandy.

Serves 4 to 6.

PECAN PIE

SHAPE   Simple Round (page 50)

FILO   About ¼ pound

FOR BRUSHING FILO

Unsalted butter, melted
1 egg, beaten (for glazing top)

FILLING

3 eggs
½ cup sugar
1 cup light corn syrup
1 tablespoon butter, melted
1 teaspoon vanilla
2½ teaspoons cider vinegar
Pinch of nutmeg
1½ cups pecan halves

TO ASSEMBLE

Beat the eggs lightly. Add the rest of the ingredients and mix well.

Continue with the folding instructions on page 50. Brush the top of the pie with a little of the beaten egg.

Bake in a 350° F. oven for 1 hour. Let the pie cool at least 1 hour before cutting it. Serve with vanilla ice cream or freshly whipped cream.

Serves 6 to 8.

LEMON CUSTARD PIE

If you like lemon, you'll love this dessert — a zesty lemon custard enclosed in crisp filo. Because the filling is so delicate, be sure to use a very sharp knife to cut the pie into serving pieces.

SHAPE   Simple Round (page 50)

FILO   About ¼ pound

FOR BRUSHING FILO

Butter, melted
1 egg yolk, beaten (for glazing top)

FILLING

1½ cups milk
⅓ cup flour
¾ cup sugar
1 tablespoon butter
2 eggs, separated, room temperature
1¼ teaspoons grated fresh lemon peel
⅓ cup freshly squeezed lemon juice

TO ASSEMBLE

Bring the milk to a boil. In another saucepan, combine the flour and the sugar over low heat. Slowly beat in the hot milk, stirring constantly with a wire whisk, until mixture boils and thickens. Remove from the heat and add the butter. Beat the egg yolks in a bowl, then add the lemon peel and juice to the yolks. Stirring constantly, slowly add the hot milk mixture to the egg yolks. Return the mixture to the pan and cook over low heat, still stirring, for about 2 minutes. Transfer to a bowl and set aside.

Beat the egg whites until stiff. When the lemon custard has cooled a bit, gently fold in the beaten egg whites.

Follow the folding instructions on page 50. Brush the top with beaten egg yolk.

Bake in a preheated 375° F. oven until golden brown, about 25 minutes. Let the pie cool about 1 hour before serving.

Serves 4 to 6.

BANANA MACADAMIA NUT CREAM PIE
HAWAIIAN

Hawaii is a special place for me, filled with many dear friends, including the artist for this book, Masayo Suzuki. Of course, I couldn't resist creating a filo dessert with some of the characteristic tastes of Hawaii.

SHAPE   Simple Round (page 50)

FILO   About ¼ pound

FOR BRUSHING FILO
Butter, melted
1 egg yolk, beaten (for glazing top)

FILLING
2 cups milk
⅓ cup flour
½ cup sugar
2 eggs, separated, room temperature
1 teaspoon vanilla
2–3 ripe bananas
¼ cup macadamia nuts, chopped
¼ cup sugar

TO ASSEMBLE

Bring the milk to a boil. In the top of a double boiler combine the flour and sugar over low heat. Slowly pour in the hot milk, stirring constantly with a wire whisk, until mixture boils and thickens. Remove from the heat. In a bowl, beat the egg yolks. Stirring constantly, slowly pour a little of the hot milk mixture into the yolks. Then stir the egg mixture into the hot milk mixture in the double boiler and cook another 2 minutes, stirring constantly. Remove from the heat and add vanilla.

Slice the bananas and add to the custard, along with the macadamia nuts. Then beat the egg whites until stiff, gradually mixing in the ¼ cup sugar. Gently fold the egg whites into the cooled custard.

Follow folding instructions on page 50. Brush the top with beaten egg yolk.

Bake in a preheated 400° F. oven until golden brown, about 25 minutes. Cool for 2 hours before cutting. Just before serving, return the pie to a hot oven for about 5 minutes to make the filo crispy again.

Serves 4 to 6.

MANDARIN ORANGE CHEESECAKE

Cheesecake works remarkably well made in filo. While you can adapt any number of cheesecake recipes, I like this one because of the essence of orange blossom water and the contrast of the bright orange segments with the creamy cheesecake and the crisp filo.

SHAPE   Square or Rectangular Pan
   (page 46)

FILO   About ½ pound

FOR BRUSHING FILO
   Unsalted butter, melted

FILLING
   1 small can mandarin oranges

   8 ounces cream cheese, room
      temperature

   1 cup ricotta cheese

   ½ cup sugar

   2 egg yolks

   1 teaspoon grated fresh orange (*or*
      lemon) peel

   1 teaspoon vanilla

SYRUP TOPPING
   ¼ cup sugar

   ¼ cup water

   1 tablespoon orange blossom water

TO ASSEMBLE
Drain the mandarin orange segments thoroughly. In a mixer bowl, combine the cream cheese, ricotta, sugar, egg yolks, grated orange peel and vanilla. Add the oranges.

Follow the folding instructions for the shape you have chosen on page 46. Bake in a preheated 350° F. oven until golden brown, about 50 minutes.

While the cheesecake is baking, prepare the syrup topping. In a saucepan, combine the sugar and water, bring to a boil and then lower the heat and simmer about 4 minutes. Remove from the heat and, when cool, add the orange blossom water.

When the cheesecake comes out of the oven, cut it into square- or diamond-shaped pieces. Spoon the cooled syrup evenly over the top. Return it to the oven for about 4 minutes. Then, let the cheesecake cool about 2 hours before serving.

Serves 6 to 8.

PAPAYA BOATS
HAWAIIAN

SHAPE   Short Roll or Boat (page 32 or 34)

FILO   About ½ pound for boat; ¼ pound for short roll

FOR BRUSHING FILO   Butter, melted

FILLING

    2 ripe papayas

    3 tablespoons or more coconut syrup

    1 tablespoon butter, melted

    2 tablespoons freshly squeezed lime juice

TOPPING

    Vanilla ice cream

    Lime wedges

    Additional coconut syrup

TO ASSEMBLE

Slice the papayas in half lengthwise. Scoop out the seeds and peel the skin. Chop into bite-size pieces and place in a bowl. Add the coconut syrup, butter and lime juice.

Follow the folding instructions for the shape you have chosen on page 32 or 34.

Bake in a 375° F. oven until golden brown, about 25 minutes. Serve hot from the oven with a scoop of ice cream in the center of each papaya boat and a lime wedge on the side. Have additional coconut syrup on the table for pouring more over the top, if desired.

Serves 4.

APPLE FRITTERS

SHAPE   Short Roll (page 32)

FILO   About ½ pound

FOR BRUSHING FILO

> Butter, melted
> 1 egg, beaten

FILLING

> 1 large firm apple, peeled

FOR DEEP-FRYING

> Light vegetable oil

TOPPING

> Sugar and cinnamon mixed together
> Freshly whipped cream

TO ASSEMBLE

Cut the apple into eighths for the filling.

Follow the folding instructions on page 32. Use your finger to seal the edge of the filo with a little of the beaten egg.

Gently place the fritters in very hot oil, a few at a time, and deep-fry on both sides until golden brown. Remove and drain excess oil on a towel. Sprinkle the tops with the sugar and cinnamon mix. Serve immediately with the whipped cream.

Serves 4.

BANANA FRITTERS
INDONESIAN

This is one of the simplest desserts in the book, inspired by the banana fritters my Indonesian friend, Artie, used to make for me.

Almost any fruit except citrus or fresh pineapple works well. Try fresh figs or papayas. Serve the fritters hot, topped with freshly whipped cream or vanilla ice cream, or both.

SHAPE   Short Roll (page 32)

FILO   About ¼ pound

FOR BRUSHING FILO
Butter, melted
1 egg, beaten

FILLING
2 medium-ripe bananas

FOR DEEP-FRYING
Light vegetable oil

TOPPING
Sugar and cinnamon mixed together
Freshly whipped cream

TO ASSEMBLE
Cut the bananas in half crosswise for the filling.

Follow the folding instructions on page 32. Use your finger to seal the edge of the filo with a little of the beaten egg. This prevents the fritters from coming open when they are deep-fried.

Gently place the fritters in very hot oil, a few at a time, and deep-fry on both sides until golden brown. Remove and drain excess oil on a towel. Sprinkle the fritters with the sugar and cinnamon mix. Serve immediately with the freshly whipped cream.

Serves 4.

MHANNSHA
MOROCCAN

Mhannsha means "coiled like a snake."

SHAPE　Large Spiral (page 39)

FILO　About ½ pound

FOR BRUSHING FILO

Unsalted butter, melted

1 egg, beaten, mixed with ¼ teaspoon cinnamon (for glazing top)

FILLING

1 pound almonds *or* 1 pound commercial almond paste

1 cup sugar

¼ pound unsalted butter, melted

½ teaspoon almond extract

½ cup rose water *or* orange blossom water

1 egg

FOR DECORATIVE GARNISH

Powdered sugar

Cinnamon

TO ASSEMBLE

Making your own almond paste is both easy and economical. Here's how to do it. First, blanch the almonds by placing them in boiling water for 1 to 2 minutes. Drain and run cold water over them briefly. Then slip the skins off and spread the almonds out on a towel to dry. When they are completely dry, put through a blender or food processor a little at a time, until they are finely ground into a paste.

Mix together the ground almonds, sugar and melted butter. Add the almond extract, rose water and egg, and mix until well blended. Chill for at least 1 hour to firm up the almond paste.

Follow the folding instructions on page 39. Brush the top of the pastry with the cinnamon-egg glaze.

Bake in a preheated 375° F. oven until golden brown, about 40 minutes. Let the pastry cool about 30 minutes before serving. Just before serving, sift a generous amount of powdered sugar on top. Sprinkle cinnamon over the sugar in a decorative pattern.

Serves 10 as a dessert or brunch dish.

Miscellaneous

GREEK-TURKISH COFFEE
MIDDLE EASTERN

Tiny cups of this intense dark coffee are traditionally served with any number of sweet/honeyed Middle Eastern pastries, including the familiar *baklava*. Made from coffee grounds so fine it is almost pulverized, it is prepared in the small, long-handled copper or brass Greek/Turkish coffeepots called *briki*. These come in different sizes, but the smaller the better, because the smaller pots will produce a beautiful *kaïmak* or foam. One never serves this coffee to a guest without the proper coating of foam on the top of each cup.

Because the sugar is boiled with the coffee, it is also customary to ask guests whether they prefer their coffee very sweet, medium-sweet or barely sweetened.

Since the coffee grounds are also served in each cup, you should allow the coffee to stand for a few minutes before drinking it, so the grounds will settle to the bottom of the cup. The coffee should be sipped slowly, being careful not to disturb the grounds.

Finally, after the coffee has been drunk, the thick grounds that remain in the bottom of the cup may be used for reading a person's fortune. I have many memories of my mother indulging in this old custom. She practiced it seriously and believed whatever she read in the cup. I, on the other hand, do it for the enjoyment of my guests.

If you would like to learn to read the coffee grounds, here's how to do it: After all the coffee has been drunk and only the thick grounds remain in the cup, take the saucer and place it over the cup. Turn the cup upside down on the saucer. Let it sit for 5 to 10 minutes without disturbing it. Then turn the cup right side up again. The grounds, which have flowed onto the sides of the cup, have created vivid images, some easily recognizable and others more obscure. The kinds of images you read in the patterns of the grounds, determined by your intuition and imagination, influence each guest's fortune. Basically, it is like reading a Rorschach test. The fortune is revealed in what the reader sees in the grounds.

Continued on next page

Here's how to make the coffee:

A 2-cup *Briki*

2 demitasse cups of water

1–2 teaspoons sugar

2 heaping teaspoons
Greek-Turkish coffee*

Place water in the *briki* and bring it to a boil. Add sugar. Mix in coffee slowly. Stir and continue boiling. As soon as a thick foam (the *kaïmak*) forms on top and the coffee boils to the rim of the *briki,* remove it immediately from the heat. In order not to break up the foam, tilt the demitasse cup and slowly pour in the coffee on the side of the cup, so that each cup is topped with the *kaïmak*.

Serves 2.

* You can buy it in tins or bags imported from the Middle East. Also, most specialty coffee stores will grind coffee beans very fine for making Greek/Turkish coffee. A blend of Arabian and French roast beans is a good choice.

Note: Egyptians often add a few crushed cardamom pods for special flavor.

MOROCCAN ORANGE SALAD

4 large navel oranges

Orange blossom water

Powdered sugar

Cinnamon

Peel the oranges, removing as much of the white pith as possible. With a very sharp knife, cut them into thin crosswise slices and arrange them on a large serving platter in a single layer. Sprinkle the slices generously with orange blossom water and dust lightly with sifted powdered sugar and cinnamon. Chill until ready to serve.

INDEX

About the Author and Illustrator

Marti Sousanis was born in Pontiac, Michigan, of Greek immigrant parents. Her childhood memories are filled with "secret" recipes for traditional Greek dishes. When she moved to California in 1963, she began delighting her friends with her cooking. Soon she was teaching classes at San Francisco cooking schools: California Street Cooking School, La Grande Bouffe and others.

Upon moving to Oregon, Miss Sousanis founded the Epicurean Cooking School in Corvallis; she then returned to San Francisco to be recipe editor of the local Farmer's Market cookbook, *Buy It Fresh* (1982). Miss Sousanis lives and teaches in San Francisco, and presently is working on a children's cookbook.

Masayo Suzuki was raised in Southern California, studied art at colleges in Long Beach, San Francisco and Hawaii, and now resides and works in Honolulu as an illustrator and graphic designer.

Cookbooks from Aris Books

The Book of Garlic by Lloyd J. Harris. The book that started America's love affair with garlic. It consolidates recipes, lore, history, medicinal concoctions and much more. "Admirably researched and well written."— Craig Claiborne in *The New York Times*. Third, revised edition: 286 pages, paper $9.95

The International Squid Cookbook by Isaac Cronin. A charming collection of recipes, curiosities and culinary information. "A culinary myopia for squid lovers."—*New York Magazine*. 96 pages, paper $6.95

Mythology and Meatballs: A Greek Island Diary/Cookbook by Daniel Spoerri. A marvelous, magical travel/gastronomic diary with fascinating recipes, anecdotes, mythologies and much more. "...a work to be savored in the reading..."—*Newsweek*. 238 pages, cloth $14.95.

The California Seafood Cookbook by Isaac Cronin, Jay Harlow and Paul Johnson. The definitive recipe and reference guide to fish and shellfish of the Pacific. It includes 150 recipes, magnificent fish illustrations, important information and more. "... one of the best manuals I have ever read..."— M.F.K. Fisher. 288 pages, cloth $18.95, paper $10.95

The Feast of the Olive: Cooking with Olives and Olive Oil by Maggie Blyth Klein. A complete recipe and reference guide to using fine olive oils and a variety of cured olives. 175 pages, cloth $16.95, paper $9.95.

To receive the above titles, send a check or money order made out to Aris Books for the amount of the book plus $1.25 postage and handling for the first title, and 75¢ for each additional title. To receive our current catalogue of new titles, send your name and address plus 50¢ for postage and handling.

Aris Books, 1635 Channing Way, Berkeley, CA 94703   (415) 843-0330